Bad things do happen; how I respond to them defines my character and the quality of my life. I can choose to sit in perpetual sadness, immobilised by the gravity of my loss, or I can choose to rise from the pain and treasure the most precious gift I have—life itself.

—Walter Anderson

Contents

Dedication

I DEDICATE THIS BOOK to you in the hope that the words, messages, exercises and support in this book will motivate you to find solace in dealing with your loss, inspire you to find your true identity and create a New Beginning for yourself. Love W.

About The Author

WILMA WROTE THIS book to help you discover a way to coping with your loss.

Wilma's own experiences in healing from her grief through the unconventional ways of using colour, writing and looking at life from a different perspective, are the basis for writing this book. She wants to help others who are struggling with bereavement to find a way to heal their pain.

Wilma believes that her inner work over the years, has helped her to gain the insight, knowledge and experience that she learned from reading and using the teachings of many authors that she respects and acknowledges. She is an international teacher, therapist and facilitator of a number of disciplines: Colour Therapy, NLP, Life Coaching, Meditation, Art Therapy, Creative Thinking and Energy Healing.

She embraces a positive outlook on life, believes that we are all unlimited if we believe in ourselves, and that we can heal from adverse experiences. She designed this unconventional combination of disciplines, to get her through the tough times of grief.

Learn more about Wilma at www.yournewbeginningbook. com

Acknowledgements

I AM GRATEFUL TO the authors and teachers who, by sharing their knowledge, experiences and teachings in their books and courses, have been an inspiration to me throughout my life. I acknowledge George Pratt & Peter Lambrou (Code to Joy), John Kehoe (Mind Power), Elizabeth Gilbert (Big Magic & Eat, Pray, Love), James Borg (Mind Power), Jorg W Knoblauch, Johannes Huger Marcus Mockler (Where is Your Lighthouse), Robert E Lesione & Marilynne Chophel (Unfinished Conversations), Gary John Bishop (Unf*ck Yourself), Theo Gimble (Healing Colour), Jonathan Dee & Lesley Taylor (Colour Therapy), Tyler Knott Gregson (Be Bold, Be Brave), Lucy MacDonald (You can be an Optimist), Thomas A Harris (I'm OK, You're OK & Staying OK) and Tony Robbins (Awaken the Giant Within) to name a few.

I acknowledge T. Harv Eker (The Spiritual Laws of Wealth), Andy Puddicombe (Headspace), Jim Dreaver (The Way of Harmony), Donna Eden & Dondi Dahlin (The Little Book of Energy Medicine), Gary Hennessey (Mindfulness Workbook) and in absentia, Napoleon Hill (Outwitting the Devil), for the spiritual work they are doing in uplifting humanity.

I acknowledge the great business minds from whom I have learned to structure my life, and am still learning, such as Sir Richard Branson, Vishal Marjoria, Matthew Kimberley, David H. Sandler, The Secret, Andy Harrington, Christine Kane, Ann Rea and Oprah Winfrey.

I acknowledge and am grateful to the souls that are no longer here—such as Nelson Mandela, Mother Theresa, Steve Jobs, Dr Wayne Dyer and Napoleon Hill - for having such a positive impact on mankind.

I acknowledge the driving energy and higher powers of the Universe for assisting me with writing this book and my journey in life.

I acknowledge my family, friends and supporters, for their belief in me and in the process of producing this book.

Finally, I acknowledge you for receiving this book and using it in the most positive way that you know.

Foreword

Dear Reader,

Your New Beginning is the book you need to read and learn about embarking onto a journey of self-discovery and self-healing after the loss of somebody close to you.

Wilma has attained several masterful skills, draws on her experiences and acquired knowledge from helping herself and others, which she imparts in a way that you can understand and apply this different approach immediately.

This motivational book has the power to help you find your true self in the light of what has happened to you. This however, requires a certain effort on your part, and the time you need to put your life back together. If you want to give your life a new direction while you are mending, you must develop new habits and internalise new ways of thinking.

Thanks to the practical instructions given in these pages, you too can become whole again and rebuild your life. Why don't you take this first, decisive step? There's no time better than today.

—Vishal Morjaria
International Speaker
Award-Winning Author

Note to the Reader & How to Use this Book

THIS BOOK IS written for information only—purely based on the opinion, personally acquired knowledge and experiences and the point of view of the author—and does not claim to provide professional advice.

It is designed with a variety of exercises—information that you may find useful in healing from loss. It provides stories and tried and trusted exercises used by people dealing with loss. It comes from an unconventional approach, recording the use of different tools used by the author as part of her process of healing. This book provides space for personal writing, unusual projects and recounts methods used to establish a unique pathway to dealing with loss. It has been set up so you can take it with you, wherever you go, as a means of using structured techniques to working through the pain.

Should you wish to apply or follow the lessons or recommendations mentioned here, you take full responsibility for your actions.

1

Why is This Book Important?

"The first step toward success is taken when you refuse to be a captive of the environment in which you first find yourself."

—Mark Caine

MY HUSBAND WAS very ill and I thought that I'd start reading up about the stages of grief. I knew that I'd have to learn about grief and loss, but he was still here and I didn't want him to die . . .

Then it happened . . . I'd been to the gym where there's no signal and went on to work from there. Just as I arrived at work, my phone beeped that I had a message. I looked at the number and called back immediately . . . I was greeted with: I'm sorry to let you know . . . your husband passed away this morning at 7 am . . . a painful knife cut right through my body—I started shaking uncontrollably, finding it hard to breathe, looking around in panic—flustered and not being able to think at all. My work colleagues saw that I was totally disorientated and asked if I was OK . . . I stammered . . . My husband's just died . . .

I hadn't wanted to talk about him dying—to him or anybody—and got annoyed when he said he would not be around for much longer. I suddenly thought: 'I should've spent more time with him last night . . . just given him one more hug . . . now it was too late . . . Well, the last thing he said to me was: "*I love you!*"

All this just faded as I had to arrange a funeral, get death certificates, sort out accounts and deal with things I had never dealt with before.

Once the initial arrangements for the funeral were completed, I found myself alone, drifting in a strange empty space, wandering, wondering what to do next.

Did I want to go to a strange centre to find somebody to talk to, as everybody was suggesting?

My husband and I had been to a few centres. They do great work there to help people. However, the talk, the hushed tones—quiet and mournful—scared me and did not lift my spirits. I had felt worse after that—afraid, depressed and very low. In fact, I didn't know anybody who'd wanted to go and discuss their feelings with these strangers. Most people I knew were going it alone.

No! . . . My mind and body shouted . . . NO!

There has to be a different way to get through this trauma . . .

I knew I had to do something different!

BUT how? I'd never experience anything like this before...

So . . . where to start, what to do, how to do it and . . .

Here I was . . . alone, emotions going crazy, having to re-discover and re-invent myself, find the strength every day to lift myself up, take one step at a time, and then start looking forward to a new phase of my life.

Having experienced this disquieting event for the first time in my life, I knew that I'd have to find a way to work through it on my own (Do not let anybody tell you that it's any different!).

For years I've been helping people work out ways to change their lives. The nearest I got to how a tragic situation like this affects people close to you, is when I gave a talk to a very large group of women who were learning how to deal with the loss of a loved one.

Now it was my turn. I had to go back and re-live that talk, but now I was on the receiving end. I decided that I had to take action to heal myself—nobody was going to do it for me.

I feel strongly that it's my responsibility to share this unconventional way of dealing with loss and grief with you. If I keep it to myself, I will neglect my duty to tell you what I have found to heal my pain. I respect, love and honour you enough to implore you to 'just do it'. If it works to you too, you'll have gained balance in finding a way forward. I ask you to believe in yourself and know that it is your time to explore and live life to the fullest, in spite of what you're feeling now. You can heal. I hope you can find solace in using this information too.

I will encourage and guide you gently through the process, step by step, if you are prepared to at least try this way. It works for me and the many others who are using this book.

I wrote this book to:

- Assure you that you will be ok.
- Offer you simple, easy-to-do 'tools' to cope.
- Guide you through meaningful activities to deal with your pain.
- See a smile on your face again.
- Show you how to re-establish balance in your life.
- Remind you that you can remember without regrets.
- Point you in a direction to re-discover yourself in a fun way.
- Answer the questions you ask.
- Explore life and create Your New Beginning.

The rest is up to you! You can help yourself to 'Be OK!'

So . . . Let's start at the very beginning!

2

Conventional vs. Unconventional

And the day came when the risk to remain tight in a bud was more painful than the risk it took to blossom.

—Anais Nin

The Phases of Grief

FIRSTLY, IF YOU want to ease the pain, the emptiness, the confusion and loss of direction, you have to start somewhere.

The 'given' starting point is to be aware and understand: you are at the back end of a huge, impactful event in your life, with repercussions and a massive knock-on effect.

Stop. Become mindful and acknowledge this. Be aware that you have to create time for yourself to deal with whatever unforeseen, strange, unexpected, dramatic experiences, feelings and questions will pop into your head and heart.

Suddenly, little memories, big memories, a song, a smell, the colour of the sky, the sound of a motorbike . . . something will come along and set off something inside . . . you can't help it . . . it just arrives and you feel that shock, disbelief and trauma all over again—you re-live this experience.

People tell you it will eventually go away . . . but it is embarrassing, untimely and unnerving.

At what point, you wonder, will your grief ever be resolved?

TAKE A STEP:

Tell yourself: 'To get through this, I have to know that it's really important to become aware and mindful of these stages or phases of grief.'

You have this book and the intention to deal with your loss in an unconventional way. Are you wondering why it seems a bit long-winded or slow with the necessary information? It's because it's a process and cannot quickly be dealt with overnight.

You'll be taken through a number of steps—some easy, some deeper, some emotional and some to energise you . . . So . . . grab a pen / pencil / colours and do these simple exercises to make it work for you too.

> The word 'stages' is about "a specific point, period, or step in the process of development". I prefer to use word 'phases' as it's meaning is softer: "a time, period in the process of change or forming part of someone's development; an informal patch; a period of temporary difficulty".

I picked a few popular descriptions of the phases of loss/grief and will refer to these throughout the book. I placed them alongside each other so you can compare and see how you are doing, which of these you are experiencing, and how you see yourself progressing.

Do This:

1. Read through the table below (each column gives you a different point of view and research)

2. Familiarise yourself with how you're feeling and what you've already gone through—this does not mean that it's done and dusted—they are all intertwined and may all happen together.

3. Be mindful and fully aware of each part of the process and that they repeat themselves when least expected!

A few quotes from researchers and therapists for your perusal:

"Grieving is a highly individual experience; there's no right or wrong way to grieve. How you grieve depends on many factors, including your personality and coping style, your life experience, your faith, and how significant the loss was to you."

"Inevitably, the grieving process takes time. Healing happens gradually; it can't be forced or hurried,

and there is no "normal" timetable for grieving. Some people start to feel better in weeks or months. For others, the grieving process is measured in years.

Whatever your grief experience, it's important to be patient with yourself and allow the process to naturally unfold."

"There's no instant fix. You might feel affected every day for about a year to 18 months after a major loss. But after this time the grief is less likely to be at the forefront of your mind."

"... eventually you will find a way to pick up the pieces and move on with your life."

Summary of the Grieving Process:

Shock & Denial	Acknowledge your pain	Express yourself
Isolation, Pain & Guilt	Accept that grief can trigger many different and unexpected emotions	Allow yourself to be sad
Frustration, Anger & Bargaining	Understand that your grieving process will be unique to you	Keep up your routine

Depression & Loneliness	Seek face-to-face support from people who care about you	Sleep
Reflection & Recognising	Support yourself emotionally by taking care of yourself physically	Reflection & Recognising. Eat healthily
Reviewing & Working Through	Recognise the difference between grief and depression	Avoid things that numb the pain—like alcohol, drugs, etc
Hope & Acceptance		Go to counselling if it feels right for you
Ref: various	Ref: helpguide.org	Ref: NHS

WOW . . . the phases of grief really opened my eyes as to what I was experiencing and made me realise that I'm not the only one going through this.

I was feeling strong most of the time. I was getting through lots of the things I was confronted with and feeling quite good—I was convinced that I was OK.

Two months later, suddenly one day I just broke down and cried and cried and cried. I could not stop. I realised that I was still reeling in a pit of emptiness, fear and insecurity.

I was not OK yet!

I tried to ignore these extreme emotions. I tried talking to people but found that I just kept feeling 'NOT OK'. I was re-hashing all this ordeal over and over, instead of progressing, releasing the pain and finding a way through it.

I read the phases again and thought: "I don't want to . . . 'eventually' find a way'. It's too vague and feels like a very drawn-out, uncertain process, without answers or healing within sight. Will just knowing this info and talking it out really assist me in coping with the inner turmoil that I'm in right now?"

From deep down inside, I seemed to find an answer to these nagging questions—NO!

I wanted to find concrete ways of healing and learning to cope—not 'hoping' for the 'eventual possibility' of getting through this. I remembered a friend who, 14 years after the passing of her husband, was still battling and *waiting* in despair to recover from her awful experience. I did not want that!

Even though I was fully aware that I'd have to be patient with myself, the sudden surges of pain, emotions, fear and uncertainty would arrive and knock me down. I knew that I had to get up again. I decided to take some action—a small step at a time, simple, do-able, specific exercises, activities, ideas, methods and creative ways that would help me to 'BE OK!'

I just knew I had to do this in an *unconventional way.*

No matter who you have lost—be it a partner, friend, parent, child or even a pet—I have used and still use a variety of approaches, presented to you throughout this book, to help others, you or somebody you know, to cope with loss and grief.

So . . . ready . . . get set . . . let's take the next step!

Right now, right here:

> *Make a decision* that you want to heal and then
>
> *choose to take action* in this process.

You deserve healing and owe it to yourself, your family and friends, your colleagues and to that person who is no longer here.

Do This:

Give yourself a score out of 10:

Give yourself a number rating your DESIRE to BE OK

after this distressing event? _____ /10

How much are you committed to using these proven ways of learning to deal with our loss? _____ /10

'I, _____ am working through
the grieving process.'

If you want this for yourself and have decided to 'just
do it', tick the box below, then sign and date your
commitment to healing.

Choose to   Take Action to heal

and   you will

                 find Your New Beginning

                 Yes—I am taking action to heal

                 Signed: _____ Date: _____

To learn more, visit: www.yournewbeginningbook.com

Defining Unconventional Ways

Let's look at what the 'conventional' ways are:

Definition: conventional: *based on, or in accordance
with what is generally done or believed; normal,
standard, regular, ordinary, usual, traditional, typical,
common.*

The advice is: 'go and talk about it to somebody'—whoever
that is. You can choose from professionals, friends, family,

strangers—somebody you feel comfortable with, or a total stranger!

Ok, that's great, but for how long do you want to talk about it? Does all this talking help you to get over it? Or does it keep the pain in focus and make you feel NOT-OK? And for how long do others want to listen to it?

Every time I spoke to somebody about it, I was doing it again and again and again. There is way more to it than just talking it away or trying to ignore it! It does not take away that frustration or the other emotions linked to your loss. In fact, it re-cycles the trauma like a raw, open wound.

Or is it about 'self-talk'?

This does not mean that 'self-talk' is pointless. In fact, it can really make a difference. The problem is that, because 'you are who you are' and your life-experiences have such a profound influence on your actions, thoughts and emotions, you could talk yourself into 'staying stuck', feeling sorry for yourself or just staying in an uncomfortable comfort zone.

Bottling it up inside is most definitely not healing either. Being harsh and saying to yourself "Oh just get over it!' . . . This does not heal.

So . . . what are these unconventional ways?

Definition: unconventional: 'not based on or conforming to what is generally done or believed'.

The concept of the unconventional way, leads you to discovering an active process to healing:

- Give yourself time.

- Understand where you come from.

- Accept and acknowledge who you really are.

- Discover your subconscious beliefs.

- Release what no longer works to your advantage.

- Set specific goals for yourself.

- Take a risk and try new, different things in life.

The unconventional methods in this book:

- Show you how to include other techniques of coping.

- Link you to your subconscious with a different approach.

- Set you up with tools for healing.

- Offer you more ways to take action.

- Provide guidelines to change the way you feel and think.

- Support you in finding a way to deal with your loss.

Why an unconventional way?

Your thoughts, beliefs, feelings, behaviour and actions are all inextricably linked. So when a formidable event 'hits you', you automatically revert to what you know from your life experiences—your thoughts, beliefs, feelings, behaviour and actions.

Are you ready to:

- Listen to your heart?

- Feel the emotions?

- Go with what is happening to you?

- Use colours?

- Get creative?

- Learn to dream again?

- Get on with your life?

. . . It's about taking ACTION!

Do This:

- Keep your mind open to doing things differently from now on.

- Make a decision to do this anyway—even if it feels a bit odd at first.

- Just Do It!

- Stick with it until you feel better.

- Be mindful of your thoughts and feelings throughout the healing process and beyond.

- Refer to the phases of grief whenever you need to.

Un-condition Your Mind

What does it mean to un-condition your mind? Tony Robbins says that: 'If you do what you've always done, you'll get what you've always gotten'. This is about 'doing'.

However, let's replace a few words: "If you think what you've always thought, you'll do what you've always done." Still rings true!

> Definition: conditioning: *bring (something) into the desired state for use.*

Your mind is conditioned to protect you and answer your self-questions. All this conditioning results in your actions becoming habits. Think about when you learned to brush your teeth or ride a bike. You no longer have to think about it—you 'Just DO It!'

WHY?

Have you recently found yourself 'just doing something' because you were conditioned to a certain way when your loved one was around, for example, thinking it's them on the phone when it rings? This is your conditioning. It's a habit and part of what you are, think and do. Well, the way to bring something 'out of the desired state for use' seems very contrary. So why would you want to change?

Because your mind is conditioned to do what you have always done—without thinking. Now that you're confronted with a painful event, you revert to what you have learned before. Your subconscious will rummage around to find something among the experiences in your life to help you cope with your loss, for example like having a tantrum, bottling it up or ignoring it and hoping it will go away.

This conditioning has taken years to become automated, a habit which comes into operation now. However, with the loss of this person, your circumstances have suddenly changed. For you to cope with the loss and heal, means that you have to change the way you feel, think, talk and behave.

I know what you are thinking now . . . NO! I don't want to change!!!

BUT . . . this heart-rending event has already changed your life.

You can choose to start the process of un-conditioning your mind in order to deal with this difficult situation you're in now—OR—or you can choose to stay in pain, misery and suffering and never really be OK.

How badly do you want to reduce your pain? Enough to do something about it? How will it affect your life if you do *not* learn to accept and make some changes? Do you feel that you're not quite strong enough to do this right now? How can you get out of your comfort zone?

Firstly, let's re-read and focus on the words of Anais Nin:

> And the day came when the risk to remain tight in a bud was more painful than the risk it took to blossom.
> – Anais Nin

How is this relevant to you and in your life?

Remember—you chose to take ACTION

So: . . . change it will be!

To learn more, visit: www.yournewbeginningbook.com

What?

Only you know right now WHAT you need and want to change.

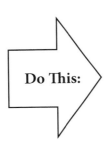

Do This:

Find a mirror and look into it. Just quietly take note of this person looking back at you—no criticism or comments. Smile at him/her and introduce yourself.

Focus on this person and ask them to truthfully answer only a few questions, then record their answers below:

1. Are you true to yourself?_____

2. Who do you mirror in your life? _____

3. Do you have something to hide? _____

4. A secret bothering you is_____

5. What are your dreams? _____

6. Are you living/achieving these dreams? _____

7. If not, why not? _____

8. What do you think is holding you back?_____

The question now is: . . . WHAT?

What do you think could be stopping **you** from coping with this unpleasant event, from being the real you and from achieving your dreams?

Think carefully about what it could be, and write as many answers as you can below:

_____   _____

_____   _____

_____   _____

_____   _____

Next step:

Look at your list above, grab your colour pens and circle the one most relevant to you right now.

1. Describe it in more detail, [e.g. I keep thinking all the time about this person not being here.]

    _____

    _____

2. Write *why* you'd like to change this, [e.g. because the sadness and pain all the time is unbearable] . . . because

    _____

    _____

Do This: Now go back to the mirror (somewhere where you are alone and cannot be heard) and tell yourself assertively that you want to change this 'blockage' and why you want to change it—be very specific and say it out loud.

To look at yourself differently means that you have to change the way you think, the way you perceive life and the way you feel about what is happening around you.

Think it's too difficult and that you can't suddenly make changes easily? Is everybody telling you that you shouldn't make decisions for a while?

When you wanted a new car, or a bag, or a couch, what did you do? How passionate were you about getting it? And did you go out and get it?

Throughout your life you've created changes, made a decision that you want something and, even though it may have taken quite a bit of effort and work, you knew what you wanted and took action to get it.

You were happy to do whatever it took to get what you wanted. See, you've proven to yourself already that if you really, really want it, you will go out and get it.

How?

Well, as you know, the details are different every time, but the underlying 'how' is exactly the same—no matter what it is that you want to change.

1. I want to change _____ ,

2. because _____ .

3. So, *HOW can* you do this?

You've guessed it . . . 'Just Do It!' . . . But, what if your 'little voices inside' are stopping you or telling you that it is too difficult and that you "can't".

Let's review buying that new car—or it can be anything else. Write what it was for you. _____

You start looking around at cars. A particular ad on TV catches your eye. You like how that makes you feel about having that car. You do some research online, check to see if you can afford it, look at plenty of pictures of the car, decide what colour would suit you, you even imagine what the neighbours will think of you.

Everywhere you go, you see this car—while driving in your old car, you see them on billboards, in the street, in the car park, around the corner—they are everywhere. The more you see them, the more you want one. You know how much you need a new car right now. You decide to go to the dealer to do a test-drive—you imagine yourself being in this car.

You arrive at the dealer, walk into the showroom and there— there in front of you—you see it. It's the exact colour you want. It's right in front of you. Before anybody even arrives to speak to you, you walk closer to your car and you . . .

- Touch it.

- You close your eyes as you smell the new interior.

- You walk slowly around it.
- You feel the beautiful shiny paint.
- You walk around it again.
- You stand as if you're having a photo taken next to your car.

Then the salesperson arrives, opens the door and invites you to sit in it and feel the comfort of the seats. You sit there taking a deep breath, smiling, elated. What a feeling! Even better than you imagined!

You get to take it for that test drive . . . And you know you have to have it!

So . . . you knew what you wanted, why you wanted it, engaged your sensory reasons, (maybe to give you an excuse to get it), added your passion for having it and you got it. 'You wanted it bad enough to get it.'

You're probably wondering what a car or 'that something' you bought has to do with dealing with grief and loss.

In the same way you applied you time, effort, desire, feelings, considerations and actions to purchasing that car, you can use this same 'energy' to 'get what you want': dealing with your loss.

You may still be wondering—How can I make this relevant to dealing with my loss?

Your emotions, thoughts, physical make-up, your perception of what's happened to you—much of it forgotten and stored in the library of your mind—cause you to feel, act, re-act and experience loss in your own personal way. (*I'll refer to these 'forgotten perceptions' as your 'subconscious'*).

Your awareness and conscious thoughts are directly affected by these forgotten perceptions. They personify as your underlying values and beliefs. You then use these automatically for survival, and you depend on them to run your life.

Even though you may think it a bit 'alternative', many ancient teachings and cultures used fairytales, stories, myths, legends and philosophies to make people aware of the role of our thoughts and the power of our minds. It's been around since the beginning of time, but many of these have been discarded or ignored over time.

Now, with so much information available and renewed studies of these old teachings and 'natural healing' (emotionally, mentally, physically, spiritually), they are re-surfacing in the form or 'mind power', NLP (Neuro-Linguistic Programming), energy and colour medicine (to name a few). These, versus the conventional medications, are becoming more popular as the unconventional way of healing today.

It is important to realise that your habitual subconscious mind has every moment of your life stored, some hidden, buried and almost impossible to recall. Your mirror knows what's deep inside—even though you may not be aware of some of these beliefs, ideas and involuntary life processes.

Whatever you think and perceive, is what you believe.

You can even change the way that you regard somebody.

For example: On a TV program bringing people together on a 'blind date', two people were matched as compatible and arrived at the venue for their date. The girl hated beards and wanted to run away when she saw him. She would never have chosen to go on a date with this particular guy—he had a huge beard.

Because this was being filmed for the program, she was expected to stay, whether she liked him or not. She struggled through it, but discovered that he was exactly the type of person she was hoping to meet as a prospective partner, that they had so much in common and that she liked him very much from the word go. She was totally surprised at how well they got on, understood each other and 'just clicked'.

By the end of the date she said: 'Never judge a bloke by the beard'.

From what must have been an unpleasant experience at a young age, she had deduced that people with beards were 'horrible' people. This had caused her to judge everybody with a beard as somebody abominable.

She was playing her own mind game.

When she met a person who had an attractive personality, was fun to be with, intelligent and caring, somebody who she was really attracted to—a person with a humongous beard—she knew that her subconscious had set her up to follow her old ideas. She decided to go out with him again because she really liked 'the person behind the beard'. Wow! Way to go, girl!

I can hear you thinking: How is this relevant to dealing with the loss of a loved one?

Awareness of the mind games you play—between your conscious and subconscious minds—is an integral part of learning to cope and deal with this upheaval in your life.

Mind Games

How do 'mind games' affect you? Why am I telling you that you are playing 'mind games' with yourself? No, I'm not judging you or trying to mess with your mind. It is a way to understand what is going on inside your head, and why you function, react and feel as you do. Do you agree? You play your own 'mind-games' all the time

Do you ever ask yourself questions like:

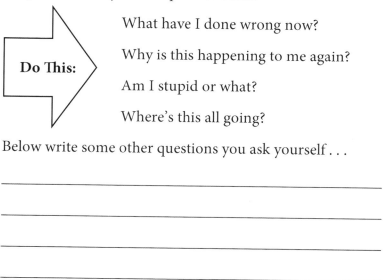

Do This:

What have I done wrong now?

Why is this happening to me again?

Am I stupid or what?

Where's this all going?

Below write some other questions you ask yourself . . .

_____

_____

_____

_____

When you ask yourself these questions, a complex procedure takes place—your mind (your subconscious) will scour through your experiences, perceptions, thoughts, values and beliefs to find an answer. It then comes up with an answer or a few options, and you feel and act accordingly.

You are playing your very own mind game!

What do you mean that's not true? Yes it is.

I can just hear you thinking: 'That's BS!" You're RIGHT . . . it is BS!

What your subconscious is handing you, is what you know from before and how you believe life to be. So—this is really your unique BS—your Belief System.

So many people talk about this. How is this created and what does it really mean?

> Definition: belief: *something that is regarded, accepted as true; an opinion or conviction.*

> Definition: system: *a combination of things or parts forming a complex or unitary whole; an assemblage of facts, principles, doctrines or the like, in a particular field of knowledge or thought; a system of philosophy.*

Since birth, your mind has stored everything that has ever happened in your life—every feeling, perception, thought, smell, taste, idea, dream, fear, colour, sound, everything you saw, heard, every touch, hug, scolding, tone of voice, fantasy, secret friend—every little detail of your life.

Here's a simple explanation of how it is set up and the impact it has on your life.

Subconsciously, you've created a library of 'existing know-how', to tap into at any time for your survival. You may not remember many of these, but when something happens to you that triggers a question or wants an answer, your mind will search through all these files and give it to you.

It will bring this past evidence into your conscious thoughts. It can only find answers from what you know, have done, have felt, have perceived and used before. Maybe it seems a bit complicated, but it is simple—you operate from what your previous experiences have taught you—this is how you function.

Still with me?

Here's an example: You go for a walk with a friend in a park where you've never been before. You're enjoying the walk, when suddenly you're engulfed in the fragrance of a plant. You stop in your tracks.

You've been transported back to a holiday you went on with your family when you were a kid. You breathe it in and remember that time, as if you're there now.

Your subconscious has recalled that lovely perfume and dumps it into your conscious thoughts—a fascinating recollection of the past right here and now—in the present.

This happens all the time, and your subconscious will remind you about the good, the bad and the ugly.

Asking yourself questions, as you do, your answers may not always be what you'd like to hear . . . but you get them anyway.

Another example: You ask yourself: ". . . Am I stupid, or what?" Your subconscious will go and find all the things that you did that were not brilliant—like taking a fall on the stage when you were getting your award at school, or that cold morning when you dropped the milk bottle and you got shouted at by your mother, and . . . You know what I mean?

Yes—you got it! These are your Mind-Games.

These questions and answers are a 'habit'—you may not be aware that you're doing this and wonder why you often get depressed, fearful, irritated, scared, angry, etc.

When you ask yourself the same questions, you *will* get the same answers.

> *Your subconscious will not question your questions—*
> *it will ALWAYS go and find an answer for you.*

If you want a different answer, you have to ask a different question. This means change.

Make a change:

Instead of asking yourself: '. . . What have I done wrong now?'

Ask yourself: 'What can I learn from this?'

You will get a totally different answer.

To change the habitual ways that you comment, talk to and question yourself, you have to become mindful and aware of your self-talk.

To instantly change your whole life, as well as your way of thinking seems quite unrealistic. You now have to deal with massive transformation, and that in itself is daunting.

But, change it is! This change—the loss of that important person in your life.

If you start moving in the direction of what you want for yourself in the future, use this opportunity to start cultivating a few other small changes in your life as part of healing from this loss.

All you need to do now is slow down a bit, be quiet and listen to yourself. Just sit patiently and listen to what you are saying to yourself. Have some fun. Smile

Do This:

Find something funny so you can have a bit of a giggle. Nobody is listening—except you. Just LAUGH!

The Process and Practice

Give yourself some time and space where you can take the first steps to change your habitual comments and questions that are part of your self-talk. Be quiet and mindful and write the first answer that comes to mind:

1. What is the question, comment to or about yourself that you use most often?

_____

_____

2. When do you usually think/say/ask this?

_____

_____

3. What response do you usually get from this to validate your behaviour or feelings?

_____

_____

4. What does the answer/comment suggest to you?

_____

_____

5. How does this answer make you feel about yourself?

_____

_____

6. What answer would you like to hear from your mind?

_____

_____

7. Think carefully now and add some sense of lifting yourself out of the doldrums and smile at what you know you can achieve:

    Re-write one question or comment to yourself which will elicit a different response. Then write it below:

    My new question/comment is: _____

    My new answer/response is: _____

Remember that you're playing a mind game with yourself—unconsciously. This one new step forward to change, means that your subconscious will be aware that you want to 'play your game' in a different way. You want to change the way you speak to yourself because you want a different outcome.

However . . .

Firstly, your subconscious is not going to allow you to change. It will not give up what it's been doing since you were born—because it is programmed to look after you and will NOT let you down.

The 'little voices' in your head are telling you that this is all foreign to you and that you don't like or want to change.

Secondly, you've been doing this all your life so far, and your subconscious will not give up nagging you and reminding you that you have habits, and that you should stick to what you know.

So . . . Here comes the unconventional—just persist at the changes you want in the same way you were determine to buy that new car.

Mind-Game with a difference:

Do This:

Make this next bit enjoyable. Smile at yourself.

Relax and know that you're moving your energy, simultaneously learning to cope with this harrowing event.

- Re-look at the most common question/comment you wrote for no. 1 above.

- Below you will see a group of shapes. As quickly as you can, pick a shape and write no.1 next to it.

- Now write this question/comment on the line just below the shape.

- Grab you colours again and colour *around* the shape.

- Decide *exactly* how you want to word your new comment or question. Check if your new answer/comment is positive. It must also have a good 'ring'. Write this CLEARLY inside that shape.

- Read it out aloud to yourself—with passion, conviction and emotion, ensuring it rolls easily off your tongue. Repeat it over and over and over, until it starts to resonate with how you want to feel about yourself. Say it slowly, mean it and tell you subconscious to take notice.

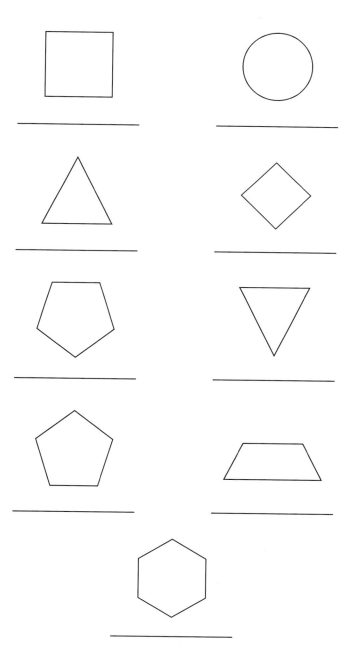

- Et Voila! Pat yourself on the back and congratulate yourself for taking this HUGE step forward.

- Now go and write it on 5 Post-It Notes and stick them up everywhere—on the bathroom mirror, the kettle, the door handle, your phone, your diary—anywhere you can see them to remind yourself of your new way of talking to yourself.

- Make a note to yourself: Repeat 5 times a day, saying it 3 consecutive times every time. Use the Post-It's to remind you, for example, below your new comment, write: 'Say it 3 times'

I know what you're thinking…

Well . . . Here's how it works . . . you have to make this a new habit!

> This next part is quite intricate, and I ask that you spend a while reading, re-reading and ensuring that you understand fully what this entails.
>
> Take your time, make sure you have some quiet time and space around you and allow yourself to delve into a deep understanding of your life up until now.

To learn more, visit: www.yournewbeginningbook.com

Make it a HABIT

What is a habit?

> Definition: habit: *an automatic reaction to a specific situation; settled or regular tendency or practice, especially one that is hard to give up; accustomed to, used to, given to, addicted to, no stranger to, not new to, inclined to.*

So far, you've had to admit to yourself that it took years to form your old habits. Habits are, once learned, stored in the subconscious for you to use, draw on and be your support. Exactly like everything else you've experienced in your life.

Unfortunately some old habits do not lift you up. This happens without thinking because . . . 'That's just me!'

The law of nature and being human, is that your subconscious has been instructed to find answers, direct your behaviour and create a pattern by which you live your life.

To change this you have to consciously:

1. Choose the exact details of that new habit.

2. Replace the old habit with instructions for the new one.

3. Think and consciously do the new, then repeat and repeat and repeat.

The bad news is that, if you think you can sit all night, chanting your new choice of words until the sun comes up, and, lo and behold, suddenly tomorrow you'll have your new habit set into your subconscious mind—Sorry! It doesn't work like that! By this time, your subconscious will know that you are planning to trick it into change and will be digging it's heels in stubbornly.

It takes at least 28 days of constantly, consistently, consciously, continuously, doing it in a different way. You have to convince your subconscious that this is what you want, that it will work better for you and tell it to acknowledge and accept your desires.

Then, the next 28 days are a bit easier and more automated. But beware—at any time, your subconscious could just let you know that the old habit is still VERY relevant in your life. Those little voices will tell you that you're wasting your time and that you should just be happy to revert to your old habit.

Do This: Demand from your subconscious: 'STOP! I want to do it this way. Remember that car! Have a tantrum 'cos you want it, and keep on and on until you have what you want. [How old were you when you started learning to get what you want?]

You know what you want, go out, have a huffy about it, and tell yourself that you have to have it! What's it like doing this again? Enjoy! Smile to yourself and make the most of it!

By the 3rd round of 28 days, you'll be surprised at how much easier it is to form this new habit.

Remember when you joined the gym? How long did you go before you gave up on creating that new habit? Or did you stick with it? Add in your passion and desire to really do it. Make sure that you make it clear to your subconscious exactly what you want and that this is your new way forward.

OK, the next step: Consider your habits.

Name 3 habits that you have currently:

    1. _____

    2. _____

    3. _____

How does each one run (or ruin) your life:

    1. _____

    2. _____

    3. _____

Name 3 new habits that you would like to have:

    1. _____

    2. _____

    3. _____

How will you benefit from each of these?

    1. _____

    2. _____

    3. _____

A house is built from bricks. Bricks are very small compared to the size of the completed building. Your habits are like bricks—small—but each one is required as an intrinsic part of a sturdy wall.

To rebuild your life, use the bricks of habit to build a strong, sturdy new beginning—one brick at a time!

Below is your progress tracker. Fill it in at the beginning of the week and tick off every day what you have done. E.g. I'm reading and working through my book Your New Beginning for 30 minutes every day.

Make this commitment to yourself:

I choose to start creating my new habit of _____ _____ right now.

I choose to do it every day for the time needed to become my New Habit and I want to continue this as my 'forever' new habit.

Date: _____ Time: _____ Place: _____

Signed: _____

The New Habit Progress Tracker

Week 1 __ / __ / __ till __ / __ / __	Day 1	Day 2	Day 3	Day 4	Day 5	Day 6	Day 7
1. Read and work thru my book YNB for _____ mins							
2.							
3.							

Week 2 __ / __ / __ till __ / __ / __	Day 1	Day 2	Day 3	Day 4	Day 5	Day 6	Day 7
1. Read and work thru my book YNB for 30 mins							
2.							
3.							

Week 3 __ / __ / __ till __ / __ / __	Day 1	Day 2	Day 3	Day 4	Day 5	Day 6	Day 7
1. Read and work thru my book YNB for 30 mins							
2.							
3.							

Week 4 __ / __ / __ till __ / __ / __	Day 1	Day 2	Day 3	Day 4	Day 5	Day 6	Day 7
1. Read and work thru my book YNB for 30 mins							
2.							
3.							

First 28 days done . . .

Week 5 __ / __ / __ till __ / __ / __	Day 1	Day 2	Day 3	Day 4	Day 5	Day 6	Day 7
1. Read and work thru my book YNB for 30 mins							
2.							
3.							

Week 6 __ / __ / __ till __ / __ / __	Day 1	Day 2	Day 3	Day 4	Day 5	Day 6	Day 7
1. Read and work thru my book YNB for 30 mins							
2.							
3.							

Week 7 __ / __ / __ till __ / __ / __	Day 1	Day 2	Day 3	Day 4	Day 5	Day 6	Day 7
1. Read and work thru my book YNB for 30 mins							
2.							
3.							

Week 8 __ / __ / __ till __ / __ / __	Day 1	Day 2	Day 3	Day 4	Day 5	Day 6	Day 7
1. Read and work thru my book YNB for 30 mins							
2.							
3.							

Write a few ideas and comments here for your own healing:

_____

_____

_____

_____

_____

_____

To learn more, visit: www.yournewbeginningbook.com

3

Alone—To Be or Not to Be . . . ?

I am not a product of my circumstances. I am a product of my decisions.

—Stephen Covey

Your Loss

THINK BACK TO a time when you lost something important—keys, a book, a special piece of jewellery.

What did you do? You started looking everywhere— maybe frantically, maybe on your own, maybe in panic, maybe becoming angry.

How did losing that make you feel then? (Write it here)

_____

If smaller, insignificant, replaceable items left you feeling like this, as you know by now, losing this person who was a part of your life results in more intense, exaggerated and exacerbated emotions and a sense of 'Now what?". Are you feeling lost—alone—afraid? All of the above and more?

It's important to learn to be mindful and aware of your circumstances, your mindset, your reactions and coping strategies.

What else have you lost with this person?

Do This:

Read all the guidelines before starting this exercise. Then set your alarm for 30 mins and Just Do It.

I suggest that you complete the whole exercise at once.

If you need more time— continue until you have finished.

Ask yourself this question: What have I lost?

Write down absolutely everything you can think of that you've lost.

Be very specific—from emotions to physical objects, time, habits and actions—positive and negative. Anything and everything! Step 1:

POSITIVE   NEGATIVE

_____   _____

_____   _____

_____   _____

_____   _____

_____   _____

Step 2:

Go back to the list above and, *ignoring* whether it is positive or negative, use a different colour pen for each.

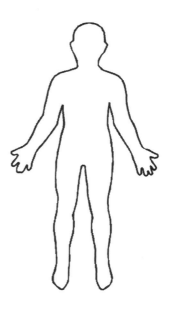

Start by circling your biggest loss and marking it as no.1. Continue circling and numbering in order until you've done them all.

Step 3:

Look at no. 1 that you circled above. Read it out aloud 3 times to yourself and focus on the feeling you have about this specific loss.

Now close your eyes and bring this feeling into your body— be fully aware of exactly where you feel it. It could be a heavy or an empty feeling.

It may take a bit of attention, but you will find the spot.

Step 4:

Using the colour you used for No.1, look at the diagram above and mark the exact spot with an X where you feel this loss.

Step 5:

Go to that feeling again. Read the details aloud to establish what type of feeling it is: stress & tension or a void & emptiness.

Step 6:

Write your score out of 10, for No1, in the chart below.

    10 = strong feeling
    0 = no emotion

Decide which is more relevant to the way it feels in your body: tense & stressed or a very empty, hollow feeling.

Take your time to do this exercise once. You can repeat it with the other losses as and when you need to.

	EMPTY /10	STRESSED TENSE /10	BIT OF BOTH /10	Name the area of the body: e.g. throat
1				
2				
3				
4				
5				
6				
7				

Step 7: (Read the instructions first. Then Just Do It!)

Sit comfortably in your chair, or you can lie down with knees bent, feet flat on the floor. Close your eyes, take your hand

and place it on the exact spot where you can feel the tension or emptiness.

Breathe in and out slowly. Pull the air in deeply at your own pace, and then let it out all the way.

As you breathe in, guide your breath to that specific area in your body. Just imagine that it's getting there. Take your time! Take gentle, relaxed, long, breaths in and slowly out.

Keeping your hand on that spot while you do this and speak to your body quietly and with care.

1 **If that spot in your body is tense** and it becomes difficult to breathe, talk to your body and ask it to release the tension as you breathe out. Make sure you take a deep, relaxed breath in; every out-breath is like a big long, long sigh—out, as if you were blowing out 100 candles.

As you breathe that stress out, allow your body to slump and feel the relief. Do this only a few times, and then tell your whole body to relax and just breathe normally until that feeling of stress has subsided. Smile as you open your eyes.

2 **If that spot in your body is empty,** as you breathe in, pretend that you're breathing in helium to make you laugh about the way you will talk. Make the helium a bright sunny yellow and smile while you think of how comical this could sound. Tell that empty space that you want it to be filled with smiles and happiness. Lift the corners of you lips as you allow the air to leave your body.

Now imagine that you're lying on a beach in the warm healing sunshine. Breathe in and out at your own pace until you feel that the empty space is filled with something that makes you happy—make sure that space is no longer empty.

Open your eyes, sit up and compliment yourself for relaxing for a few minutes. You deserve it and you owe it to yourself.

Do This:

NEXT time:

Whenever you have that painful spot in your body, clarify whether it is tense or empty. Re-read the guidelines and do this breathing technique to release that feeling.

To learn more, visit: www.yournewbeginningbook.com

The Memories

Now that you've lost this special person in your life, you realise that you're alone. However, what you have for the rest of your life are the happy memories of your time together.

If you are overwhelmed with extreme sadness, you can turn this emotion into happy memories—is this not a better way to live?

If people are telling you to 'get over it', this does not mean— "Just forget!" If that is what you think it means, think again.

Even if you think you will or can 'forget'—I have news for you!

You will NEVER forget, because those memories are stored in your subconscious. What you can change, though, is your reaction to your loss.

Yes, there are unpleasant memories too—ones that you'd like to forget—but they will always be there. Do you think your loved one would want you focus on these dark, painful memories? If you could ask them, how do you think they would like you to remember them? Write it here _____

_____

You're confronted with 2 different options now:

1. Remember all the pain of your loss and stay on a journey of inner destruction.

   Or

2. You can focus on the happy times and turn your overall reminiscences into joyful and fond reflections.

Do you think your loved one would want you to live in misery—never healing from this tragic event?

Do you feel that you have to keep your memories alive to the extent that they are always causing you pain and stopping you from healing?

Other people may be telling you (or you may be telling yourself), to keep the memories alive. The problem is that memories kept *alive* can play havoc with your emotions and push you into a hole.

How can you get out of the hole without these intensely severe feelings of loss, sadness, etc? If this is painful every time, around every corner, everywhere you go, whatever you do, you will not be able to deal with your loss. It will 'eventually' turn on you, causing physical and mental distress. Do you want to live a never-ending story of 'I can't cope'?

Somebody I know, who was struggling for many years to come to terms and deal with her loss, kept saying: 'I don't want to forget him'. Exactly, I completely agree.

Nobody can do that! Remember, everything you have experienced in your life is ingrained into your subconscious and cannot be removed. Your loved one's time is stored there for the rest of your life.

You really only have 2 choices again:

1. Either you live in the past, being sad, miserable, regretful, lonely and heartbroken for the rest of your life.

   OR

2. Or you can acknowledge that you were given time with this person to live, learn and experience life together. It's time now for you to keep these memories safe and joyous, while continuing to re-build your life.

Ok, so that seems a bit harsh…well, that depends on how much you believe in yourself, your self-esteem and self-value and how much you want to heal.

Do you think you deserve to be happy again? That you are valuable and valued enough to enjoy life to the fullest? Are you giving yourself permission to take your life back?

Do This:

Here's how you can focus on keeping the memories in a positive way, steering away from pain and sadness and remembering the good times:

Create a 'Happy Memories' Tribute

1. Create a designated 'special space / place' that you want to use for your "Happy Memories". Get a special box with a lid or an album. It will keep it free of dust. It has to provide a private place to keep everything together, that others can't disturb. Your loved one deserves something special, and so do you. Make sure it's big enough for all the items you'd like to put inside, and decide where you'd like to store it.

2. Find photos, words, a watch, a ring, a mug . . . things that bring memories of the good times—even a poem or a letter that you want to write to them—you can always add more later.

3. Do a little celebration ceremony. Decide exactly when, what, and how. Choose who will be there to take part. If you are inviting others, find a suitable time for them too. Then write it into your diary, prepare and collect everything you need to

make it special—you can even include music. Get
it all ready before the time.

4. When the time arrives, if are others are joining
    you, let them know how you plan to have this
    celebration. Start the music, pick up each item,
    talk about it, 'dedicate' it to the HAPPY memory
    you want to remember. Touch, feel, look at, smell,
    listen to, even a little kiss if you want on each
    item, as you gently place it into your special box.
    A few tears of sadness and joy are OK too. Find
    your own way with words and feelings to do this.
    As you place each cherished item into the box,
    acknowledge and thank this person for leaving
    you these wonderful memories.

5. Once you've placed the last item in the box,
    infuse cheerful, grateful feelings over them all
    and imagine that it is filling up with love and
    'happiness' until it is full to the brim.

6. Pick up the lid and, as you start to place it over
    the top, say a special Thank You to this person
    for being a part of your life and send gratitude to
    them as you close the box.

7. Place it somewhere safe and easy to get to, for
    example on a bookshelf, in honour of these
    memories.

Whenever you feel that you want to remember the exciting
times and lift yourself from a surge of painful emotions,
open your special remembrance box. Be sure to remember

only the happy times, happy thoughts, happy emotions and happy memories.

Repeat whenever, to transform your sadness into positive memories.

Keep these memories happy—by retrospectively changing any self-destructive thoughts, to fond reminders of the time shared here on earth with this person. Then acknowledge and honour the privilege of having these wonderful memories.

Gratitude

You've just created a special memory box—a reminder of the good times you had together. I also know that you are probably wondering why you are looking at 'gratitude' now.

Well, as you are alone and possibly feeling that life is not fair for 'taking your loved one' at this time and age, you may be feeling very low.

I'm sure that lots of people have told you that you can change this all by just thinking positive thoughts and with 'positive talk'. Well, that in itself doesn't really work. Not just talking anyway—and you have your subconscious, throwing all your experiences and perceptions at you, underlined by your beliefs, (Your BS!).

However, there is a way that you can re-direct your subconscious to be more positive, just by changing your focus.

While you focus on the negative, the difficult, the bad, the sad or the painful parts of your life, what you've lost and your agony, you *will* stay stuck in that place.

Instead, force yourself to look at life in a different way. Look at the bright side of life.

Yes, OK!—I get your point—all the positive talk and the positive thinking can't change what has happened and you're left to deal with life on your own now—without this person . . .

So . . . What does gratitude have to do with coping with loss?

> Or the fact that you are dealing with imminent hardship now?

> Or that you have to learn how to be alone?

> Or . . . .

It has EVERYTHING to do with all the above.

Do This:

This is why I want to share this 'Gratitude Attitude Circle' with you.

Doing this regularly—at least once a week—can make a profound difference to your *'pain and suffering'* (please remove these 2 words from your dictionary!)

Being grateful is part of the unconventional way of changing how you think and perceive your life.

You, like me and everybody else on the planet, take many things for granted.

NO! I'm not telling you off—It's just like this: If you go and make a cup of coffee before you leave the house because that's just what you do, you are taking for granted that you have coffee, a mug, a kettle, electricity, sugar, a teaspoon, in your usual mug or take out with you—your first cup of the day! Get the picture?

What the GRATITUDE ATTITUDE CIRCLE does is this:

. . . It Changes Your Focus

From feeling terrible, sorry for yourself and 'taking life for granted'

To finding a positive way to look at things.

- Acknowledge what you have been taking for granted.
- Appreciate what you have.
- See life from a different perspective.
- Create happy thoughts, feelings and insight.
- Understand that you are OK.
- Love, honour and respect yourself.
- Know that you can cope with the loss of that special person in your life.

In the shape below, write all the things that you are grateful for:

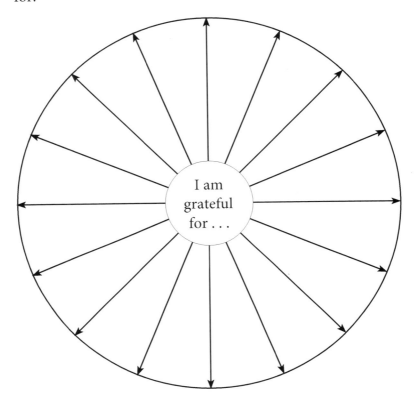

I am grateful for . . .

It will probably not take long to fill the circle. Draw these every day and fill them with the tiniest things you can find for which you can be grateful. If you find that you are repeating yourself after a few days, start the next day with writing one down with the reason you are grateful, e.g. Today I am grateful for the rain, *because* it helps the lawn to be lovely and green.

Find and enjoy all the little things you took for granted and lift your spirits.

To learn more, visit: www.yournewbeginningbook.com

Alone vs. Lonely

You may find your first few months quite busy: people around you and supporting you, other people shocked at the news, the return of all the things that have to be sorted out—like when you get a letter from the bank or that your MOT has expired, and on and on . . .

During this time you may be very aware that you are alone.

No matter if this person was your partner, parent, sibling, child, another family member or a close friend, being alone becomes strikingly intense when you have to sort out the electricity tripping or a burst water pipe, or doing what you haven't had to sort out by yourself before.

Do you automatically turn to ask them something, pick up the phone to call or get in your car to drive there? Or do you look at your watch and expect them to walk through the door? If you want to discuss a problem or ask what they think, or take two cups out of the cupboard, you suddenly realise that they're not there.

Whatever your relationship was with this person, the anguish returns in a flash as you realise the truth—you are alone.

A person I know whose parents had passed on when she was quite young, had both her sisters die unexpectedly within two months of each other. She said to me: 'I'm an orphan now!'

What a way to feel! What a perception to have!

That vivid reality check comes from your subconscious mind—it could be triggered by a memory, a smell, a sound, a habit—and it's real. You've lost the person you could talk to about making decisions, the one you would chat to over a cuppa or a drink together, or just sitting quietly watching TV.

What a gap, an empty part of your life, a huge void. Let nobody kid you—it takes some getting used to.

Write here what 'alone' means to you. _____

_____

This 'being alone' isolation is one aspect of loss that you have to deal with. If it's causing you to feel insecure, frustrated, angry, anxious and even depressed, it is undeniable, there is no other way.

It is what it is.

You have to embrace the fact that you're strong enough to get through this phase of your life.

There are ways you can work through this, but let's first look at the other side of the coin: Being Lonely

Loneliness creeps up on you long after the first shockwaves have subsided. You get to a place where you know that you're working through and dealing with the loss and trying to get your life together . . .

Then—your supportive people have left, everybody around you has resumed their usual lives, you've managed to accept and understand that you are alone, you're aware that there's a way forward, feeling really OK!—when, waiting for the bus or in the dentist's room or just flicking through the TV channels, it slowly sinks in that you are lonely!

It takes a while to process the impact of your loss and the painful understanding of what this really means to you.

From the 'lonely' point of view, what impact has this loss had on your life?

_____

_____

Alone is a definitive.

Loneliness is derived and prompted from your perceptions— your subconscious. You can be alone but not lonely. Loneliness arrives from a different angle and sometimes unnoticed. When that link/bond is no longer there, the loneliness can be overbearing.

There's a subtle difference between **alone** and **lonely,** as there is a subtle difference between **bond** and **link**.

The bond you had, is not so much physical, but a connection on a subconscious level: talking, listening, knowing and a feeling of togetherness.

The link with your loved one is more about of the things you did together, the chats, the phone calls, your habits and the items you still have as a reminder. It's more of a physical connection.

To come to terms with being alone, here are a few ways to break that habitual and emotional link with this person— Don't worry!

The *link* (stored in your Special Memory Box) will remind you that you have a *bond* with your loved one.

You need to create a habit of being alone.

A

This specially-designed exercise can help you to re-condition your mind, to get energised and help you change the habit of having that person around.

Due to the fact that you cannot bring them back, it is advisable to break habits that link your routines with the things that you did together. This helps you to opt for healing and to fill the empty space that this person filled.

Do as many or all of these. Take your time.

When something triggers an emotional flood or a pang of pain and sadness, do one of these to break the habit of having them around. Then create a new habit to replace the old.

Make this a new habit!

1. Sit in a different chair in the lounge.

2. Change where you would normally sit at the table.

3. Sleep on the other side of the bed.

4. Sleep the wrong way round on the bed—pile up your pillows at the foot end of the bed, move the sheets so you can get in and do 'wrong-way-round sleeping—even if it feels strange—just do it.

5. Sleep in a different room sometimes or for a few nights.

6. Change the ring tone on your phone.

7. Rearrange the furniture throughout the house if you can.

8. Take the dog on a different walking route.

9. Park the other way round in the driveway.

10. Re-decorate.

11. Do something creative—paint, sing, dance, arrange flowers, write a book.

12. Join a class or club—something you wanted to do for a long time—learn to play golf, learn a new language.

13. Move your favourite TV watching chair to a different place.

14. Cook something completely different.

15. Change the place where you put things in the fridge.

16. Take a different route to work.

17. Walk backwards to your doorway—be careful please!

18. Use a different coffee cup.

19. *Write your own ideas here:* _____

_____

_____

B

If you meet others who are 'in the same boat as you', you will realise that you are not the only person having to learn to deal the loss of a loved one.

You may want to join a group of like-minded people—do some research or ask around—there will be a local group that you can go to. There are many support groups for people who have lost a loved one.

Be aware that they could host people who are not doing what you are learning in this book. My friend went to a group near her, but found it rather depressing. She said that there was so much crying, that some of the people were just not ready to move forward with healing the pain and sadness. This does not mean that all the groups will be like this. Find one and try it, and see if it would work for you.

Alternatively, or additionally, I have started an online support group for people who are using this book.

To learn more, visit: www.yournewbeginningbook.com

Belief = Perception = Reality

So you are aware that change is a huge part of what you are doing in your life right now. You are alone and have to get on with your life.

If you were a constant support for this person before they passed on, the impact will be very pronounced. You may not be aware of it, but their dependence on you worked both ways—so now you have to deal not only the loss but your constant 'having to be there' for them.

You know how much time and effort you used and, when this person isn't there, even though expected, you were still in shock. You may have to think about: 'What do I do with myself and my time now?', because you were constantly focused on their needs. You may also feel free now that you no longer have somebody depending on you to do so much. This is all ok! Be mindful of these and revise what role you want to take on now.

If your loved one took his/her own life, the impact on you and all the people who knew this person, will be substantial and extreme. You will also have many un-answered questions, most of them not in your subconscious mind. This is dealt with in Chapter 8 pg 179.

If your loved one died suddenly, the shock will leave a different heart-wrenching hole in your heart and your life. The perspective changes a bit.

What you believe about them and yourself will influence how you learn to cope. You will also have many un-answered questions, most of them not in your subconscious mind.

You are here now, probably wondering how to step forward and deal with your loss.

What you believe about your loss and what you subconscious is giving you, and how you perceive your situation, is directly linked to how you are coping or not.

Write an honest answer to each:

1. What do you believe about your life right now?

   __I believe _____

2. What do you believe you could have done more of before the passing of your loved one?

   __I believe _____

3. What do you believe happens after death?

   __I believe _____

4. What do you believe about this person passing on?

   __I believe _____

5. What do you believe is the reason for this trauma in your life?

    __I believe _____

6. What do you believe about yourself in dealing with this dramatic event?

    __I believe _____

7. What do you believe you can learn from this experience?

    __I believe _____

8. Who do you believe should 'take care of you'?

    __I believe _____

9. Who do you believe you should 'take care of'?

    __I believe _____

10. What do you believe about your future?

    __I believe _____

11. What are you afraid of? (Ref Ch 4.3 Pg 91)

    __I'm afraid of _____

12. What do you believe you can do now?

    __I believe _____

13. Do you believe that you can re-construct your life if you choose to? _____

Write, sign and date your intention below:

I _____ believe that
I can re-construct my life by _____
_____
_____

starting today, (date)_____

Signed: _____

Now that you have looked at what you believe and your impression of where you are in your life, the 'burden' of your loss may be a bit clearer and lighter. Go back to each question and see if this perception is different to your belief. If it is, make a note of it and decide how you want to approach each of these aspects of your life.

In short, what you perceive your life to be is your reality. No arguing that.

So the question here is: Are there a few more 'perceptions' that you would like to change. Create the specific details and add them to your habit tracker in Chapter 2 Pg 39.

You are Not Alone

Who are you talking to? Who is guiding you to mourning in the way they think you should? You will find that some people, whom you least expected, will be there to support you—thank them and value their care. But they will have to leave—they have their own lives—and you will find yourself alone.

Who is pushing you to what they think you should or should not be doing? Are you allowing yourself to be manipulated by some people who think that they know what is best for you?

What about those you feel are reliable and that you are connected to? That's fine for a time, but they also have their lives and families and will need to allow you to get on with your own healing.

Some people, that you spoke to before, will just disappear off your radar—into thin air. And you thought that they were your friends and support!

Others will just be in your way and over-talk, over-question, or ignore speaking about it altogether—so . . .

Take some action and decide who you want around, who you don't, then let them know that this is your time to work through your loss.

You are probably thinking now that I'm contradicting myself—I keep saying that you are not alone.

Well, depending on what you believe, you are a part of nature. Nature is part of you. If you believe that you can reach out to your higher self, God, a higher source, the universe— whatever works for you—you can make that connection to know that you are not alone. Just as your loved one can be there for you to talk to, know that they are around if you would like them to be.

You can talk out loud to whom-ever you choose—even if it's just out loud. Just imagine that they are there and know that, by talking and writing, you can connect with a higher 'force' that will support you, and that you are not alone.

4

Emotions

Don't judge each day by the harvest you reap but by the seeds that you plant.

—Robert Louis Stevenson

Defining Emotions

OMG, THE EMOTIONAL roller coaster is huge! It's fast, it's furious, it's scary, inconsistent and unexpected.

Emotions defined: *strong feelings deriving from one's circumstances, mood, or relationships with others; an affective state of consciousness in which joy, sorrow, fear, hate, or the like, is experienced; any strong agitation of the feelings actuated by an experience and usually accompanied by certain physiological changes, as increased heartbeat or respiration, and often overt manifestation, as crying or shaking.*

Are you experiencing massive emotional episodes? Especially soon after this has happened to you? The confusion about being alone or wanting to have others around is real and daunting, leaving a feeling in unsure-ity (if there is such a word).

One minute you want to be surrounded by people and almost afraid to be alone. The next minute you feel claustrophobic, with too many people around, wanting to talk to you, asking you how you are and giving advice—and you just want to be alone.

>>> EMOTION 1: "I just *don't want to be alone* right now!"

When this strange sensation envelops you and the panic of being alone becomes overwhelming, just to be near others—even if not to talk to—will help you restore some balance for yourself. If you have an animal around, bring them closer and play with them, and get them to interact with you. If you feel you want to get an animal for company, it may be a good idea to follow up on this.

Do This: Get your shoes on, grab your wallet and take yourself out to the closest coffee shop and treat yourself to a cuppa. Take a book or a magazine, a crossword puzzle or the newspaper, or even this book. Then just sit there, enjoy not being on your own and involve yourself in that activity you brought. Do it NOW!

Set your alarm for about 2 hours and decide what you can do when you get back e.g. tidy out a drawer and decide which shoes you are taking to the charity shop.

Simply sit there and 'people watch'. This helps to give you that sense that you are not alone. Be *really mindful of what you are thinking while you are out. Consider the facts—you are surrounded by people—this means that you are not alone. Tell yourself that you just want to watch and enjoy the fact that you're quietly sitting on the side, observing. It's your treat.*

Warning: do not go out 'drinking'—alcohol will stop you from being mindful and will delay the healing process. It will also just numb your sense of being with people. You can 'take a rain check' for another day. If you've done this once, take yourself somewhere else next time.

When you get back home, get straight on with the little task you set yourself. Do it quickly and then congratulate yourself for being so amazing. Can you start feeling the release of unwanted emotions and a slight (maybe a huge) surge of energy?

OR . . .

>>> EMOTION 2: "I just *want to be alone* right now".

Do This: Set your alarm for 2 hours. Decide quickly where you can be alone and what you will do after you've had this time. Get some water to drink (or a warm cuppa). Find a place where you will not be disturbed— you want to be alone and deserve this time—If there are others in your house, let them know that nobody is allowed to disturb you for the next 2 hours, then close your door for privacy! If you are going out to a park or for a walk somewhere beautiful, make sure you take a blanket to sit or lie on and your journal and a pen.

This alone-time is for you to allow your emotions to take over completely. If you are finding it difficult to know what and how to use this time, just do whatever comes to you. *Remember, your subconscious can help you find out what you need now—curling up under your duvet, a sleep, a cry, writing, screaming into your pillow, standing under the shower, crying as the water washes over you.*

Release the emotional tension, sadness, questions, frustrations, anger, pain and expectations. Every time you do this, different emotions will come up. It is soooo healing! Let it all out, and when your alarm goes off, acknowledge your healing, stop, smile and stand tall.

You're done now, so get straight on with the small task you set yourself. Do it quickly and then congratulate yourself for doing so well. Be mindful that you are releasing some of those unwanted emotions and a slight (maybe a huge) surge of energy.

Every minute of the day, become present and aware of your emotional status. Once you have been able to create the habit of being mindful of your present moment, you may be able to prevent an embarrassing episode if your emotions decide to take over. It happens without warning.

Before this event in your life, what were your emotions like? Have you always been very emotional, or have you always kept a stern control?

Is this how you are now too, or has something changed?

__same / different __

Mark which best describes how you feel:

1. <u>If you are extremely emotional</u>:

   - How do you feel during an emotional 'moment/outburst?

__embarrassed / __couldn't be bothered / __somebody will feel sorry for me / it's ok but I remove myself from others __.

- How do you feel after an emotional 'moment/ outburst'?

  __ better / worse __

- What do you do to stop this wave of 'emotions'?

  __ it just goes away / _____ I have to force myself to stop / _____it just runs out of steam / I can stop it suddenly and pretend it didn't happen __

2. <u>If you have your emotions under control and feel that you're strong and keeping it together':,</u>

   - How do you do keep your emotions at bay?

     __ take a breath and stop myself from crying / hold my stomach tight till they go away __.

   - If you feel emotions, what happens to them?

     __ they just sit in my body / ___ totally numb / I don't have emotions __.

   - What irritates you the most about people who 'can't control their emotions'?

     ___the lack of control / __ the noises they make / __the embarrassment of the emotions / excessive attention seeking behaviour __.

You may be in denial but you have to accept that you have emotions. You may express them in a different way and perceive them from a different viewpoint than people who are 'emotional'. That's OK! You still need to be mindful of what emotions you are feeling and then acknowledge that you have them.

What feelings do you have inside that are controlled emotions? Numbness / neutrality / annoyance / _____.

Emotions are an integral part of your make-up, like it or not. You will experience them in different proportions in your life—remember they are linked directly to your subconscious.

Your life consists of different aspects: physical, mental, creative, spiritual, and emotional, all making up the whole you.

How's your Maths—never mind—just do this one . . .

Rate how you feel about each of these aspects of your life right now. Give each one a score out of 10—the Maths trick here is that, when adding them all up, you are only allowed to have a score of 10.

Have Fun!

Physical	_____
Mental	_____
Creative	_____
Spiritual	_____
Emotional	_____
Self Value	_____
TOTAL:	_ 10 _

Using the percentages above, create your own pie chart in the circle below.

Write the name (physical, mental, creative, spiritual, self-value and emotional) in each section, draw the size of the pie about the same as the percentage (%) and then colour each part of the pie a different colour.

Write today's date next to your pie chart so you can monitor your progress. This may change considerably as you work through the healing process.

Now that you understand yourself a bit better, decide what changes you want to make. If for example, physically you are very low, decide when you want to go for a walk, where and how long you will walk. Then just go and do it!

Here's an example:

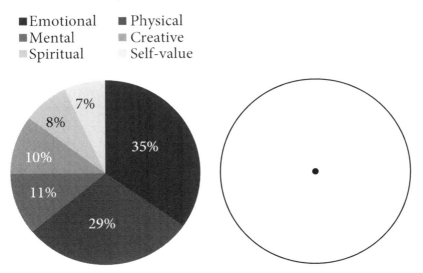

Write what you can do to improve each of the aspects of your life:

Physical   _____

Mental   _____

Creative   _____

Spiritual   _____

Emotional _____

Self-Value _____

To learn more, visit: www.yournewbeginningbook.com

Overwhelm vs. Balance

"I can't help myself—I just start crying!"

I was going away for a bit, a few months after my husband had died. I felt I needed to just get away. I realised that I had been on a whirlwind road leading nowhere, with no healing in sight and I was still confused, angry, frustrated and needing a break. I had to go somewhere near the sea, and wanted to keep it on a small budget. I found a brilliant solution. I was flying to a warm country and was excited, hoping to have a refreshing, re-energising, 'finding-myself adventure'.

I'd gone through the phases of grief, listened to what people had told me would happen and what I should do. I was proud that I was actually doing something to help me deal with my loss and 'get over it'.

I was nervous going to a place on my own, but had friends close by, who I knew would be there for me if I fell apart. I was excited, yet not sure of what lay ahead. One thing I knew was that I was healing quickly. I was 'strong and in control'. I was OK!

Or so I thought!

We were on the runway and speeding up for take-off . . . and OMG, what a take-off that was.

With every inch we climbed into the air, 5 000 tears descended from each of my eyes—there was no stopping them. Luckily my hair was long enough to pull forward across my face, to try and hide what was happening. Worse still—I was squashed in between two total strangers.

I wanted it to be over, but I just couldn't stop crying. I couldn't get up because we were far from reaching the height when the seat-belt lights would go off—we were still climbing.

I tried to distract myself by peering inconspicuously past the passenger next to me, to look out of the window. At the first glimpse of the blue sky, my eyes just decided to dive in really deep and swim under water.

There was no relief, nothing I could do. And then, as I can't breathe under water, my body followed suit. I sobbed uncontrollably—so violently and so embarrassingly that I had to take a large tissue (fortunately I had some in my pocket), open it as best I could—I couldn't really see what I was doing—cover my face completely with the tissue, hold my hand over my whole face, cross my arms and grip the arm-rest with the other hand to brace myself, This didn't stop the deluge. I had no control.

Victoria Falls came gushing out over my face and reduced my tissue to a sloppy, wet blob in my hand. Those awful wailing sobs vibrated through my trembling body, the snorting as my nose decided to join in the exhibition—I created an embarrassment of note.

This continued all the way—the whole trip—one and a half hours of it—until I heard the announcement to fasten our seat-belts. We were about to land.

Suddenly, something weird happened. It just stopped, as quickly as it had arrived. It just disappeared! . . . Wow!

I still can't explain it—I had clearly moved pent-up emotions. I was in another country, had missed the excitement of the view and had embarrassingly and unintentionally disturbed the trip for my fellow passengers.

I was about to embark on a 'get-over-it' trip.

I had not known what to expect . . . But this? What a way to start my journey.

At least now I can smile—well—have a good laugh about it! Those poor people on either side of me!

I sure hope that you've not had quite such an embarrassing experience.

What's happened to you? _____

How did you feel after the 'episode'?_____

I've had a few more episodes where I'd just start crying, without warning, without reason . . . but hey, this is part of it. After each of these 'emotional times' I would feel lighter, have a bit more clarity about who I am and remember that I am still healing from the ordeal I felt I'm in.

So, if you are doing anything as wild as this—that's brilliant! I know it will help you to heal!

Here are a few exercises to transform your overwhelm to finding some balance.

Do This:

Read through the guidelines first, then do each of the exercises.

A

Find a place where you can be alone with your emotions—get a box of tissues and allow yourself the time to cry . . . Do not judge yourself . . . just be emotional.

Make sure you are warm and have lots of water to drink. Be aware that this is a large part of your healing. Honour yourself by giving yourself the time to do this. [Please Note: Your writing is for your eyes only]

When you're ready, grab your laptop or journal and start writing. Just write and write and write—through the tears, the sobbing. Just keep writing your feelings, your thoughts, anything and everything that comes to mind. Write until you feel the pain, the sadness, anger, frustration, fear and uncertainty easing a little—take however long you need. Do not feel guilty about the time, or think that you have to stop.

You won't read it again. It's not going to be read by anybody else. No fancy literary style—just write as quick as you can. Talk as if they can or cannot hear you—whichever works best for you. You need to 'say' it to them. Get it all out as if they have to be quiet and listen to you now. This is how you start releasing the emotional tension and questions and move toward healing from the shock of your loss.

Every time you do this, different emotions will come up.

B

Once you've finished,

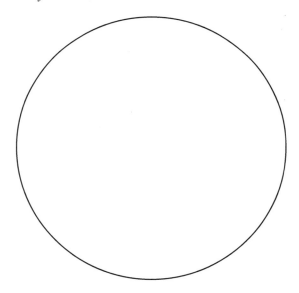

Colour this circle green

Do This:

C

Before you start, read these guidelines carefully. Read and record the visualisation in the box below, then listen to it and follow the steps. Talking as you record it and then listening and doing it, are all part of the healing process.

[When you read to record it—read it quietly and very slowly as if you are talking to a person and helping them to be calm and relaxed. Stop, relax and pause between sentences—there is no rush. Keep a low tone of voice, soothing the listener to relaxation. You can be your own calming influence. [Watch out for those little subconscious voices!]

If you've never done anything like this before, it's ok. Just try it!

Close your eyes and imagine that you're sitting in the middle of this green circle. Make it just the right size so you can touch the edges with your hands. Imagine that you reach out and pick up the edges, pulling them gently up over your head. Where your hands touch above your head, close the circle to form a ball of soft green light surrounding you, soothing your pain. Keep your fingers touching for a few seconds to seal in the light and make sure it stays like that. Ask it to stay around for as long as you need it. Feel the tranquil warmth of the green light enveloping you as you relax your arms at your side.

Slowly feel the green permeating your body. Feel the warmth on your shoulders. As you lift and drop your shoulders to relax them, the gentle colour comes in to soften the tension. It softly flows down your arms to your hands and fingers. Move them just a bit to allow the green light to fill your fingers. Feel it touching your skin.

Your shoulders are relaxed as the green light touches and soothes your throat and caresses your upper back. You can feel it inside your chest, bringing serenity to your organs and peace to your aching heart.

Slowly, breathe in the green light - a long deep breath into the deepest part of your lungs - allow the green light to soothe your heart and your body. Then be aware of the air leaving your body as you breathe out through your mouth. Hold it for a few seconds while you relax.

Pull the green air back in through your nose again, and, as it drifts through your body all the way down to your toes, it starts to change colour. It becomes a beautiful turquoise colour. Enjoy the energy of this turquoise in your body and warming your skin. Your awareness changes the colour to a deeper blue - a warm sky-blue you'd feel when you're lying on the beach. It reminds you of serenity and peace. Just enjoy breathing this beautiful sky in and out as you relax. Allow quiet, comfortable, slow breaths to drift in and out.

Become mindful of how this colour makes you feel. Be aware that it is restoring quietness and a calm inside that you really want for yourself. Just feel and be in this soothing space.

Just be. Be here now, be tranquil, be neutral, and be at ease. Be in harmony with the exquisite blue surrounding you and within. Be restful, composed, relaxed, quiet and unruffled. Just know that you are supported by this wonderful blue. Just Be.

Hold this feeling in and around you until you feel calm . . .

When you are ready, take one last deep breath of wonderful blue . . . and as you breathe out . . . gently open your eyes.

Sit comfortably in a chair, your back supported, feet flat on the floor, hands relaxed and comfortable. Press play:

Whenever you need to release any intense emotions, or just want to feel more relaxed, repeat this visualisation exercise— as often as you'd like. You've got the recording now.

If you are new to this and feel that somebody else should to read it for you, you can listen to it on the website at www. yournewbeginningbook.com

D

Read the instructions first and then do this energy-balancing exercise.

You can do this outside if it suits you.

Sit in a comfortable chair with both feet flat on the floor. Make sure that your back is supported by the back of the chair. Raise your head up at your crown so it feels like you are straightening your spine. Shake your shoulders to loosen any tension.

1. Once you are comfortable, cross your left ankle over your right one.

2. Touch your right shoulder with your left hand, and drop your elbow so that your arm is relaxed but holding it across your body.

3. Touching your left shoulder with your right hand, relax your right arm crossed over the left. Hold them crossed but relaxed in this position.

4. Close your eyes and focus on your breathing. As you take a long deep breath in through your nose, touch your tongue onto the roof of your mouth, and, as you breathe out through your mouth, relax and drop your tongue so it rests on the bottom of your mouth between your teeth.

5. Do this for a few minutes until you feel the tension leaving your body and you are relaxed.

6. When you are ready, open your eyes slowly and be aware of the relaxation you have just experienced, and take that feeling with you.

"What if I just can't or don't want to cry?"

So, you're not doing the emotional thing, because crying is not what you do. Ok, fair enough! Everybody has to deal with loss in their own way.

After a horrible, dramatic and traumatic divorce, my son seemed to be coping very well with the fact that his father was not around and did not contact him often. I was really concerned and worried about how he was dealing with the loss—but he seemed to be OK!

Then one day he came to me and told me he wanted to play ice hockey. I looked at him and wondered how this had popped up as something he wanted to do—he wasn't interested in playing aggressive, contact sports like rugby. There were a few reasons, he told me. I then looked at him and told him that it was a very rough game and I thought he would not be 'angry and aggressive' enough for the game. He just said: "Watch Me!" I did.

He went out on that ice and played with a vengeance. I was very surprised and it made me realise that this was one of the ways he was dealing with and getting rid of emotions still lingering and bothering him from the divorce. Without him realising it, his subconscious was urging him to get rid of his emotions in this way.

Even if you're not the crying type, there are emotions that you need to deal with and release. Your view and experience of how you express your emotions is unique to you—find a way and allow yourself to heal.

If you've just not been able to cry, even though you think and feel that maybe you should cry, something may be blocking your emotions and making it more difficult to deal with and work through this experience. It could have a negative impact on your health and body much later.

If this is you . . . let's explore some possible reasons:

Write your answers to these questions:

1. The reason why I think I can't cry is because _____

      _____

2. I don't think I need to cry because _____

      _____

3. I believe that if I cried _____

      _____

4. I believe that if I don't cry _____

      _____

5. If people cry, I _____

Crying is not the only way you can express and release emotions.

Have you found out yet why you are not crying?

Here are a few ideas to release your emotions and transform yourself by finding balance.

E

For this exercise you may need a bit more planning and time. You know that song, by Tears for Fears: listen to it and sing along (it's on the internet).

> Shout
> Shout
> Let it all out
> These are the things I can do without
> Come on
> I'm talking to you
> Come on
> Shout
> Shout
> Let it all out

Well, this is a brilliant way to get rid of any emotional baggage or trauma. Find a place far away from people—you don't want to alarm anybody.

Look for a very large park, a forest, a beach, go to an area where people don't know you . . . once you've found a place . . . just SHOUT, SHOUT . . . let it all out.

Shout to move the stress and tension. Shout to release those emotions that you may be struggling with.

E

Join a club—take up boxing or a sport where you can vent your feelings. Strong emotions should be released, instead of staying pent-up inside. Whatever you cannot or do not want to express, will manifest in some form of self-destruction and disease in your body. For your own health and well-being, learn to deal with your emotions—Take Action!

F

If you feel you want to let out your emotions and cry but find it really difficult—here are a few more options: Find a time and place where you are alone.

1. Watch a sad movie—this may be just the way to get the tears started.

2. Look at photographs and focus on the memories—feel the sadness of the loss—focus on the pain of this person not being here.

3. Go to a place where you and your loved one spent time together. Sit there and imagine that you're having a conversation with them. Tell them how sad you are that they are no longer here with you. Be really sad and try to allow yourself to cry. Make sure you are there alone.

4. Again find a place where you do not have an audience, and *rant*. Yes, give yourself free reign

to say anything you want—a bit like Speaker's Corner. Put yourself on a stage if that helps and rant. From deep inside, say what you want to say with passion, moving you arms and body to emphasise just how strongly you feel—and rant, rant, rant. Do not stop until you've said what you want to.

Raise your voice and make yourself heard. Go for it! Rant, rage, express with passion until you feel that you've said everything you think needs to be said.

Then, once you're done, sit quietly, breathe in and congratulate yourself for getting that all out. Close your eyes for a while just to become quiet and calm after that huge adrenalin rush. Become mindful that you've just done yourself a huge favour—you've released a shed-load of those emotions. Feeling better?

FEARS

Definition: Fear: *a distressing emotion aroused by impending danger, evil, pain, etc. whether the threat is real or imagined; the feeling or condition of being afraid.*

When I was really small, I had absolutely no fear of heights. I would stand on top of walls or high places where I could look straight down. I'd climb to the very top of pine trees on the plantation near our house, hold on with one hand, the other swinging through the air as if I was a bird, enjoying the view. I loved being high-up because it made me feel free. No fear.

When I was about 6 years old, we were invited to celebrate, with our friends next door, the start of their first ever holiday cruise. We went to see them off, along with quite a few other neighbours. I was enjoying my first visit to the harbour, in my own world, standing right on the edge of the pier, looking down into the water at my reflection way down below.

Our neighbourhood bully, a big fat nasty boy, was also there. He came up to me from behind and suddenly pushed me. He obviously knew he'd be in trouble if I fell in, so he had grabbed hold of my clothes. I felt myself falling forward, and then with a big shock, he yanked me back and started laughing at me. The shock of that incident was so huge that from then on I was terrified of heights—until way into adulthood.

No, I had not actually fallen in, but the reality of being off-balance, that falling forward partly over the edge, the physical feeling of instability and the realisation that there was a potential danger for me in being so close to the edge—even the wind could have blown me into the water—created my fear of heights. From then on my subconscious mind told me not to get too close to the edges because it could mean potential danger. My fear of heights had become excessive, to the point of embarrassment on many occasions. This story has a very good ending, though.

During an extremely uncomfortable incident as an adult, when I couldn't move because of my fear of heights, something magical happened.

I'd gone on a hike with a group of people, most of them strangers to me. We were going to find a beautiful, hidden waterfall, far into the mountains. A long slender wooden deck, about five metres long, was built out over the edge of the rocks, enabling people to see the water cascading down a steep ravine. The only way to see it, was to walk out onto this deck—out 'into the sky'.

I heard the people in front of me gasping in awe at the exquisite beauty of the colour of the water and their exclamations of wonder at seeing, hearing and feeling the spray of this special presentation of nature.

There was another lady a few steps behind me and I froze in panic. I was terrified that she'd get too close and prod me to walk closer at the waterfall. I stopped, stood with my feet apart, trying not to fall over. I was about ten metres from where the walkway started. I was petrified and couldn't breathe or move—my usual reaction when close to a high edge. Thank goodness she had stopped too—I was safe for the moment. The adrenalin has set in, and when I could move my head slightly to monitor the status of her proximity to me, from the corner of my eye I could see her—frozen, panicked and cowering. She was doing exactly the same as me! In fact, she had done what only my pride had stopped me from doing. She had dropped to the floor and was sitting in a sorry-full state, saying: 'I can't go there! I can't do that!"

My subconscious mind had told me to freeze, but had omitted to let me know how absolutely stupid it looked.

I took one look at her, saw my reflection in her and decided to walk out onto that deck. I deleted that fear in an instant. I didn't like what I saw in that 'mirror'. I chose to delete my fear and to fix it. What a splendid waterfall! One not seen by many people.

See, magic can happen, but you have to make the magic.

I know what all the self-help books, the motivational speakers, the coaches, therapists and trainers teach you.

FEAR is False Evidence Appearing Real.

Well, **forget that!** That is too way out, too strange and . . .

- Maybe some of your fears are because of what really happened to you when you were young.

- If, at a young vulnerable age, you were told that something bad would happen to you, and you believed it, it would have become a fear.

- If an unthinking adult or older person had pretended to frighten you with a spider, that could have caused you to be terrified of spiders from that moment forward.

- Or you saw a film that was meant to scare you into never going into a graveyard at night. So your subconscious told you it was real, causing you to fear graveyards at night and everything you associated with it—even the music that was playing in that scary film.

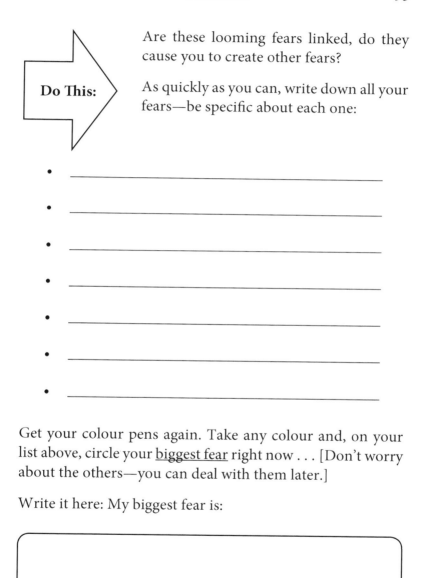

Do This:

Are these looming fears linked, do they cause you to create other fears?

As quickly as you can, write down all your fears—be specific about each one:

- _____

- _____

- _____

- _____

- _____

- _____

- _____

Get your colour pens again. Take any colour and, on your list above, circle your <u>biggest fear</u> right now . . . [Don't worry about the others—you can deal with them later.]

Write it here: My biggest fear is:

Use a different colour. Write in this box how realistic or true it is. Then write what you can do to fix or change it:

Now look at what you know you can do. You have planted the seed of self-belief, of confidence and trust in yourself. Acknowledge it, re-read it, nourish it and keep repeating it to yourself. Make it grow. See! You can do it!

Time for action:

Step 1: Sign Below!

Wow, today, I made a decision to get rid of the fear of _____

_____.

I feel good and confident that I can.

Step 2: Write down your next action: _____.

_____.

Step 3: Do it.

Step 4: Record here what you did and when _____.

_____.

When you are ready to tackle the next fear:

Repeat steps 2–4

Record what & when it was done _____.

_____.

Repeat with any of your fears when you are confronted with them.

Make this a new habit. Ref Chapter 2.6 Pg 35

To learn more, visit: www.yournewbeginningbook.com

All Those Questions

Over and above your emotions—the questions come flooding in—yes—that's what happens to you and everybody else who is going through this.

Do This:

Revise your self-questioning and how to address this in Chapter 2.4 pg 25

For you to create a resource that you can refer to when situations come up again, instead of your usual negative or uncertain answers from your subconscious, use these answers to remind yourself that you want to change.

Write the first answer that comes to mind for each question:

Refer to your answers when all the questions come rushing at you again.

What lesson can I learn from this upheaval in my life?

_____

What are all the good/positive things I did before this person passed on?

_____

What impact did my life have on this person?

_____

What did I learn from this person?

_____

What can I do differently now?

_____

Why do I think this happened?

_____

What can I do to accept this situation?

_____

What can I do now to heal from the pain?

_____

What can I do to help my close family?

_____

(Optional) How am I helping (e.g. my children)
_____ to cope / understand and find a
way to deal with this loss? _____

_____

Who can I talk to? _____

_____

Write your own questions and answers below:

_____

_____

Your answers to these questions can help you when you're
stuck.

You may even want to change some of your answers—do
that now—it's part of the change for your healing. Refer to
them at any time.

To learn more, visit: www.yournewbeginningbook.com

Pain—Guilt—Blame—Regret

Yes—it's natural to feel all of these: pain, guilt, blame, regret
and many more—at any given time!

PART 1:

As quickly as you can, write down all the things that have triggered emotional 'incidents' from time to time in your life.

_____

_____

_____

_____

_____

_____

_____

Grab a colour again and circle the first one that jumps at you.

In the table below, fill in columns 1 and 2 for trigger one only.

[Do the others later when you are ready—you only need to take one little step now—one trigger only. You can keep adding more at any time, as and when you become aware of them, and you will.]

1. One <u>trigger</u> that cause feelings of guilt / regret / blame / anger, etc.

    Be very specific: *e.g. a motorbike speeds past me while I'm driving on the motorway*

2. In the 2nd column, <u>name your feelings</u> and <u>why</u> you think you are feeling this.

Be very specific: e.g. *Sadness; wish I could be on that bike now—my husband and I did lots of great bike trips and I miss that.*

1 Triggers	2 EXACT feelings and WHY you feel like this…
1	
2	
3	
4	
5	

PART 2:

You are now going to link the trigger to a shape.

Re-read trigger 1 a few times, then VERY QUICKLY pick a shape below that you see first. Write no. 1 inside it. Colour it whatever colour you feel.

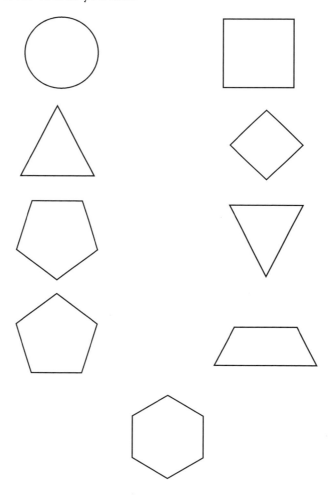

PART 2 a:

If you feel up to it now, circle and number the triggers on your list above, write them into the shapes and colour. You can go back to the columns at a later date.

Picking the shape that fits with each 'trigger' for you and then colouring it, helps to change and balance the energy around each emotion.

Do This:

Whenever something triggers that over-whelming feeling again, come back to this page, find the shape that you chose and focus on it for about a minute.

Then quickly close your eyes and keep the shape and colour in your minds-eye until it disappears.

Gently open your eyes and be mindful that you are in the process of healing. Breathe in, a big sigh out and SMILE!

PART 3:

Start again with the first trigger you wrote in Part 1 above.

Think about the conversation you'd have about this with the person who's no longer here. Tell them what you are feeling now, and just talk to them.

	Dear _____ (name of person), I want you to know that . . . (write your answers without reservation ...)
1	
2	
3	
4	
5	

Re-visit each trigger as you do them—now or at a later date—and then write a conversation about each.

Frustration vs. Action

What are you finding frustrating? With the huge number of things that you have to do now that you never had to deal with before, whatever you are confronted with—the shock, the frustration it's OK! To feel frustrated and angry now that you have to cope with all these things—well—you may want to have a rant about it. That's OK!

Rant for a bit—that's good—Go for it! Let it all out!

You know that song (I Get Knocked Down)—by Chumbawamba? Sing it to your heart's content.

I get knocked down, but I get up again
You are never gonna keep me down
I get knocked down, but I get up again
You are never gonna keep me down
I get knocked down, but I get up again
You are never gonna keep me down
I get knocked down, but I get up again
You are never gonna keep me down

Sing it loudly so that it reverberates throughout the house. You will be amazed at how you feel when you sing this over and over, every time you get knocked down.

This is a great way to make yourself get up again, especially when you suddenly feel despondent and wonder if you have the strength to do it.

The story below, reminds us that, no matter what happens, we can get up again, we can find the strength to do what we need to do—to deal with anything in life—not only the loss.

The Story of The Little Blue Engine.

Take yourself to a valley surrounded by tall, lofty mountains. Nestled at the bottom, on the only horizontal plane, is a modest village with a historic train station—a junction where all the passengers have to gather to be taken to their destinations. Travellers are transported, in comfort, to the heights for skiing and walking holidays. This is also the only way to get food supplies and all things necessary to these remote areas.

The only way up to the peaks is by train. At this station, the carriages are prepared and the locomotives serviced, to ensure that they are in top form to take the sightseers all the way up the extremely steep mountain sides.

During this busy festive season, the rail engineer technicians have much to contend with. They have to ensure that the locomotives are in good running order. The Little Blue Engine, who is almost just big enough to push and shunt the massive locomotives to the front of the carriages before ascending into the peaks, is running his little wheels off. He's painted a beautiful blue colour, resulting in being applauded by onlookers, so he does his lowly work with pride. He is barely bigger than the boiler of the smallest locomotive. He admires the strong locomotives and the people who live in the fresh air, with stunning views, at the top of the mountains. He has never been up there and is not built to climb those heights. He is content with his life here in the junction. He knows that his work is the cog in transporting the thousands of people to their holiday havens.

It's a cold winter's day, the 24th of December. With the first showers of snow—eager, excited holidaymakers are waiting to be taken to the top of the mountains—the resorts and trains are fully booked. To get their passengers to their elevated destinations before Christmas eve', everybody is working overtime, doing double shifts. The locomotives are rather exhausted, overworked and cold, yet they are doing their best to accommodate all the guests.

Suddenly, the largest of the locomotives starts coughing, sneezing and spluttering. He takes an extra drink of water to alleviate the flu symptoms that he has had for a few days. He realises that getting ill is untimely and imminent. He is scheduled to be the last run up the mountain before midnight—then everybody will be off for Christmas Day. At least he will have time to recover.

Alas, he cannot deflect getting sick. Within an hour, he is completely unable to take a breath deep enough to start up the fire inside, let alone consider going up the mountain. And then there are the six carriages, filled with presents for the children living and on holiday in the mountains, to be pulled up the arduous mountainside behind him. As the Little Blue Engine arrives to shunt him into his usual space in front of the carriages, he looks down, eyes blurred from the symptoms, and has to break the bad news that he cannot make this trip. The Little Blue Engine tries to encourage him, but when he starts to cough uncontrollably, his fate is sealed. The last train has to be cancelled.

The Little Blue Engine manoeuvres his way around to see what would have been taken on this last trip before the special day. He looks inside and sees all the beautifully wrapped gifts, waiting to be delivered. He is very upset and sad—all those presents—NO! He cannot bear to think how disappointed all the children will be if they do not get any Christmas presents. He goes back to the big locomotive to ask him if he could possibly try one last trip. He sees him slumped over, eyes dribbling, nose pouring and looking dreary. It is clear that he doesn't have the strength to move, let alone take presents to the hopeful children. He wonders what he can do.

He thinks to himself, "I wonder if I can do it? All the other locomotives are away and will not be back in time. There is only one option!"

He looks around and takes a long drink of water, stuffs as much coal as he can possibly fit into his coal storage compartment and makes his way to where he would normally push the large locomotive to be attached to the carriages. He smiles to himself. As he backs up to the front of the carriages and wiggles himself ready to be connected, the engineer asks him what he is doing. With a big grin, he tells the story and asks to be hooked up. The engineer verbalises loudly how worried he is about the Little Blue Engine's decision. But…

Teeny-weeny flurries of steam start popping out of the Little Blue Engine's chimney. He takes a deep breath and puffs up his chest to make more steam. He flexes his muscles, checks to see that his wheels are steady and says loudly to the engineer: "I think I can!" By uttering these words, he feels a surge of positive motivation. He says it again and feels the hint of movement. He says it again, and realises that he can talk himself up the slopes. "I think I can. I think I can. I think I can!" Slowly but surely his wheels start rolling on the tracks. He is moving — with the six carriages behind him. This inspires him to say this again, and again and again.

The rhythm of what he is saying, sounding like the chug of the large locomotives, is becoming steady. With this resounding chug of "I think I can, I think I can!" repeatedly, he starts advancing up the mountain, all the while saying this over and over and over. In some places where it is much more difficult, he says it with more passion and keeps moving upwards. He knows it is a long way, but he persists until he can see the lights of the station at the top of the mountain. Pushing as hard as he knows he can, he is relieved to be able to slow down and stop at the platform, where Santa is waiting to receive the gifts.

Wow! He did something he had never done before—out of pure determination.

He proudly thinks to himself: "I thought I could, I thought I could!" as he rests for a few minutes. Once the carriages have been emptied, he shunts himself to the other side so he can head back down. As he starts to prepared for the descent, he happily chugs to the tune of: "I knew I could, I knew I could, I knew I could."

Below, on the left side, write your list of things that you have to do that you wouldn't have had to do before . . . Then, once you have a list, write what you think you can do to solve this.

To Do   I think I can . . .

_____   _____

_____   _____

_____   _____

_____   _____

_____   _____

_____   _____

Get yourself some brightly coloured Post-It notes, and write three things to do on each one. Number each in order of priority. Stick them where you can see them to remind yourself. Tick off each item as you complete it. You can do it!

Be that Little Blue Engine—think you can, know you can, put the energy into it, get up again and get it done and then know that you could!

The See-Saw

Do you feel like you are on a see-saw?

Remember when you were learning to read:

Up, Up, Up.
Jane goes up, up, up.
Down, down, down.
Tom goes down, down, down.

Is this how you feel sometimes? Absolutely! Like me, I'm sure you've discovered that life's a bit like a seesaw now. All seems fine and it's up, then not-so-fine, and it's down.

Did you like to see-saw in the park with your friends? Did you like to balance and see how long you could stay suspended in the air? Did you ever fall off? Did you go flying through the air? Remember landing with a bump? And did you survive? Did you sometimes stand up on the middle and seesaw alone?

Throughout this process of healing and learning to deal and cope with your loss, there will be many times when you fall off, or go flying through the air, or just sit there balancing gently on your see-saw of life. There will be times when you land with a thud on the ground—and that hurts. And there are times when just have your see-saw to yourself.

The opposite of up is down.

Do This:

In the space provided below, write your feelings—all underneath each other.

Find some emotions and feelings that you're experiencing now and write them below: words that describe your feelings, how you feel about yourself, describing your loved one, how you are coping, how you want to feel, how you are feeling about your loss, about your future, about people around you, about the family, your situation right now. Whatever words come to mind.

Once done, go back to your list and write their opposites in the other column.

_____   _____

_____   _____

_____   _____

_____   _____

_____   _____

_____   _____

_____   _____

Use the see-saw effect to get yourself out of a hole and into a happy, contented place,

Get the orange colour pen and circle all the positive words. Use this list to lift yourself up and have 'fun in the park'.

Remember, wherever there is a down, there is always the opposite: get up again, think you can, know you can and then pat yourself on the back and say: 'I knew I could'!

Be mindful of your thoughts > > > Acknowledge each one.

Monitor every thought > > > Let it go if it sends you flying into emotional upset.

Write it down > > > Hold on tight, re-write it to get a different answer.

When emotions take over > > > let it out, sing, write and find the balance.

When you are alone > > > get up, stand in the middle and proudly see-saw by yourself.

Stand tall in the middle of your see-saw and balance—one leg at a time—put your arms up in the air, take a deep breath in and feel like you are a kid again.

To learn more, visit: www.yournewbeginningbook.com

5

Discover Yourself

I refuse to accept other people's ideas of happiness for me. As if there's a one-size-fits-all standard for happiness.

—Kanye West

Looking Outside

YOU'RE SURROUNDED BY your environment: nature, buildings, weather, people: family and friends, work colleagues, strangers, people you don't want to be with, teachers, educators . . .

When you were born, you had to find out what life was about. You developed in your unique way and learned everything—through your environment, your senses, through what you were told to do, how to behave and what and how you should be as an adult. You built fears through exposure and involvement in your surroundings, what you refused to accept and you took on systems that you were told were the way of life. You are you because these became your truth and your reality. If there were things that hurt you, you were none the wiser, accepted what happened and created your own BS.

As you started developing, you started doing things by yourself, asking questions and even wondering why certain things happened the way they did.

These were out of your control and you did not have the capacity to change painful experiences that didn't work for you. However, tantrums helped you to get your own way! Things were done to you, for you and around you that created your beliefs and trust in other people, in yourself, in your way of doing things, your outlook on life's situations and how to interact with others. How you thought you should 'be' was influenced by your environment. As you grew into a teenager, your questions may or may not have been answered, your independence may or may not have been stifled, your rebellion showed that you no longer wanted to be controlled and told what to do—you started doing more and more of what you wanted to do and be (or maybe you just did what you thought way the way things had to be done). (Phew!)

Don't kid yourself though. If you think that who you are now is just who you really are, think again.

Fortunately or unfortunately, before you could break free from depending on others for your food, your water, a warm bed, a roof over your head, deciding what to wear and who your friends were, you were a *direct product of your up-bringing.* You could not do anything about that—you were too young to understand reasoning ability as your life was mostly recorded in visual learning. But your coping strategies and interpretations of what happened then —that only arrived much later in your life.

What a way to start life on this planet!

During the first 7 years of your life—without exception— you learned some of 'the good, the bad and the ugly'. Every single person has experienced some of each. And to remind you—it is ALL stored in your subconscious.

A number of people did or said something to you which is engrained into your subconscious mind—something that still has an impact on your life today.

Do This:

It's all in your subconscious, just sit quietly and ask your mind to recollect and remind you of some incidents that made you who you are: their names, what the situation was, what they said or did and what you got from this

The next few pages of writing are for your eyes only. Write without limits and say what you need to say:

PART 1

Write the name of every person who had a great influence on your life, and what you learned from them—the good, the bad and the ugly:

Name of Person	What they said or did	Your age more or less	What you learned from this = What you have come to believe because of this.

PART 2

What overall effect has this had on your life? Write about it, how it makes you feel and how you now see this person.

PART 3

There will be some amazing and really unhappy and 'ugly' experiences in your life, things that you heard, or that were said and done to you that still make you annoyed, angry, hurt, frustrated or excited, confident and courageous—which helped you to be successful.

Write a short letter to each of these people, having a conversation with them, thanking them for the lessons they taught you . . . or letting them know that they really hurt, confused or caused you to have a difficult time. Write to each of them, do not hold anything back.

Once you have finished all the letters, take the ones where you have spoken your mind about the unhappy 'ugly' experiences, and go and burn or shred them. As you do this, speak to this person and let them know that you do not accept what they said or did to you and want to get it out of your life by burning or shredding it—tell them that you want to destroy that bad memory this way. As the flames rise into the sky—say good-bye to those unpleasant emotions.

If you have any letters of gratitude, you can either send them to the people if you can (make a copy for yourself first), or keep them so you can go back and remind yourself of the wonderful, positive influence that person had on your life.

SO . . .

How does looking outside affect the way you perceive yourself right now? How does it make you see yourself as, who and where you are?

As you ponder on these questions and answers, I'm sure you realise that it is important to discover who you really are. Well, I want to re-phrase that—it is important to re-discover who you really are.

If you know this and feel that you are really living your true self, that is wonderful, and congratulations. If this perilous event has thrown you a bit of a curve-ball, maybe just maybe there are still a few aspects of who you are that you'd like to re-consider and review.

Who Are You?

After my husband passed on, in the midst of me trying to sort out my life, establish what I wanted and to find out who I am, my son said to me: You used to be very different before—I remember what you were like—but you changed. I really hope that you'll get back to enjoying life, that energetic, amazing you that you used to be.

In the back of my mind I knew this, but right now, I wanted my mojo back and had no idea where it was. I had to do some serious inner questioning and digging to find out who I am, what had happened to me and where I could find 'me' again.

You, too, will be doing some serious digging so you can find yourself amongst all the debris of your experiences in life, including this last major crisis. Like an onion has many layers to it, you will start with the outer layers.

Just be truthful here—remember this is for your eyes only.

(Just write as much as you need to and then score your feelings.)

How <u>were</u> you feeling about yourself whilst your loved one was here?

_____

_____

_____

_____ / 10

How has this <u>changed</u> since the death of your loved one?

_____

_____

_____

How are you feeling about yourself right <u>now</u>? _____ / 10

Do This: ➡

Read the part 1 guidelines below then . . .

'Just Do It!'

PART 1—*You can do this here or on larger paper. HAVE FUN!*

1. Draw a picture of yourself / your life right now (do not colour it)!

    (It's OK—this is not an art lesson and nobody will see it—the reason to draw instead of write, is to get in touch with yourself on a different plane).

2. Add in some details of your environment, family, friends, anything 'great' & 'not great'— EVERYTHING

3. Include adjectives and words onto your drawing, describing how you feel about—the 'good, the bad and the ugly'

PART 2

1. Re-look at your picture. CIRCLE the 'not great' things and <u>cross them out</u> (within the circle).

2. Get your colours and colour the rest of the picture—all the things that make you happy, that you like and make you feel good about yourself.

KEEP THIS WHERE YOU CAN LOOK AT IT REGULARLY

Now write a few words about what you want your life to be like now—whatever comes to mind first. Just write.

_____

_____

_____

How are you feeling now? _____ / 10

Do This:

1. Next, write a letter to yourself.

    Congratulate <u>yourself</u> on how well you are doing right now—put today's date on it!

2. When done, fold it up, put it into an envelope, seal it and write your name on it.

3. Take the sealed envelope and find a place to hide it . . . a drawer, a box, a bookshelf, a book—somewhere out of the way.

4. Forget about it . . . one day you will find it and see the progress you have made.

Be a Kid Again

Today, or as soon as you can, make an appointment with yourself—set yourself some time. Then go to a special place, just be there and DREAM!

Do This:

Close your eyes and pretend that you are a kid again. Go to your favourite place. Sit there and imagine and remember. [Ask your subconscious to bring back some of these memories]. Even if it takes a while, choose to re-live a fun/enjoyable childhood experience. Listen to the sounds, smell the fragrances and immerse yourself into the feeling of freedom to dream big. Take yourself back to that time. It's all in your memory and there to recall if you want to. Make a few notes to help you to fill in the details below.

E.g. your special paintings, your pet, your secret friend, your favourite toy, what you wanted to be when you grow up, a dream.

If you are struggling with this you can find more information on www.yournewbeginningbook.com

Write into column 2 exactly what you can remember:

what you were thinking, feeling and believing about yourself then:

1	2	3
1 Your specific dream(s). [e.g. I want to be an artist when I grow up and stand and paint outside on an easel]		
2 Your feelings, dreams of how you would be when you grow up. [e.g. I am connected with nature and want to paint them to hang on the walls in the house]		
3 What you believed about yourself then. [e.g. I believe that I am a well-known artist selling my art for lots of money.]		

4 What did you think other people would think of you, how would they see you? [e.g. people would want to have my art on their walls]		
5 Write down in detail what you were doing [e.g. drawing lots of pictures of gardens, flowers, bugs, mountains, the sea—because I want to be an artist]		

Next: In Column 3 give yourself a score out of 10 for achieving today exactly what you dreamed about then.

How have your dreams, visions, beliefs and feelings about each of these changed?

1. _____

2. _____

3. _____

4. _____

5. _____

What's happened is that, as you grew up and got on with life, your beliefs in 'who you are and what you are', became fixed—fixed into your subconscious as to how you should 'do life'.

As you continued your development and growth into who you are right now, these became you values.

> Definition: value: *the importance, worth, usefulness, merit, effectiveness, significance of something; code of behaviour, rules of conduct; principles or standards of behaviour; one's judgement of what is important in life :"they internalise their parents' rules and values as passed on to us as children".*

Revisit each of the above points and re-write them as you feel about them now—today!

1 Specific Dreams		
2 Feelings about 1		
3 Self-belief		
4 What will others think?		

5 Actions		
6 Your Values today		

What have you re-discovered about yourself?

Note as many positive things about yourself as you can in 10 minutes:

_____

_____

_____

_____

_____

_____

_____

_____

_____

_____

Timeline

History is often measured or shown on a time line. We can learn from history. Your life until now is history, and you can learn from your history.

Below you will draw up your own time line of your life.

Write all significant details that you can remember into the years indicated. Be sure to include any turning points in your life. Use a black biro / ball-point pen.

The top row will show the highs and the bottom row the lows. The middle line is a neutral time that you can recall.

0-7 yrs	8-14	15-21	22-28	29-35	36-42	43-49	50-56	57-63	64-70

Now that you have filled in the events of your life on your timeline, take 5 different light-colour pens. Dark ones will not work as you still want to see the writing underneath.

Pick the first colour to mark your emotions.

Over top of the writing, mark with little crosses the age where your highs and lows were for your emotions around each event that you can remember. Highs can go up to 10/10 and lows down to -10/10, e.g. when your cat died, you were devastated and emotionally felt -8/10, and when you got that special toy from Santa, you were on a 10/10.

Now draw a curved line starting at 1 year and keeping your pen running from the first cross to the next, link every one, going up or down, as if you are trailing your emotions through every year throughout your life. It will look a bit like polygraph test readout.

Then take a different colour and do the same for the physical aspect of your life, e.g. you broke your leg so you couldn't go on that hike. Got it?

Next, in a different colour draw your line about money, e.g. when you lost the change after buying milk at the shop and you got into trouble because your mother thought you had spent it on sweets.

Then your work, career and lastly your creativity.

Was there a particular incident where they all coincided?

This helps you to link with your subconscious so that you can bring these stored memories into your conscious thoughts.

It will open your mind to get a better understanding of what has made you who you really are.

Looking Inside

To figure out just what impact some of the milestones in your life had on you, choose one incident that stands out clearly—one that was unpleasant and hurtful, one that you can still remember.

I'll give you an example of such an incident in my life, then you can get on with yours:

My mother had thrown away my favourite doll—a rag doll— because she said it was dirty and looked awful. When I started protesting about what she did, she told me if I protested any more, she would give me a hiding. I still remember it clearly. She had taken it from my toy box without telling me and decided that I should no longer be allowed to play with this particular doll (amongst quite a few other toys). What I learned from this—then at this vulnerable age—was that I had no right to make decisions regarding my possessions. I was controlled by others and had to accept it without argument.

It took me a lot of digging to realise why I was thinking, behaving and expecting others to take charge of important things in my life. I learned that this is not true and that I can change how I see myself and what I do.

Now it's your turn:

1

_____

2

_____

3

_____

How do you feel now that you're more aware of the smallest things that had a huge impact on your life?

BE MINDFUL of these and become aware of who you are and who you want to be.

To learn more, visit: www.yournewbeginningbook.com

On the Surface

Questions to think about and bring to the surface, who you are.

1. The happiest moment of my life was

   _____.

2. My greatest fear is

   _____.

3. The trait I deplore the most is

_____.

4. My biggest extravagance until now is

_____.

5. The most interesting journey I've done is

_____.

6. I feel really old when

_____.

7. My true love is

_____.

8. I'm the most happy when

_____.

9. The talent I would most like to have is

_____.

10. My current state of mind is

_____.

11. My greatest achievement has been

_____.

12. The lowest depth of despair was

_____.

13. My favourite occupation is

_____.

14. I believe my best feature is

_____.

15. What I most value in my friends is

_____.

16. My favourite writer is

_____.

17. My favourite celebrity is

_____.

18. The real hero's in my life are

_____.

19. I most dislike

_____.

20. I would like

_____.

21. My motto in life is

_____.

A Deeper Look at Yourself

Three considerations—just write whatever comes into your head:

1. I am . . .

2. The negative feedback I got . . .

3. The positive feedback I got . . .

To learn more, visit: www.yournewbeginningbook.com

6

Your Strengths

When I let go of what I am, I become what I might be.

—Lao Tzu

Your Needs

NOW THAT YOU know yourself a little better, it is time to consider your needs, how you perceive them to be, and what you need to do to ensure that they are met.

Firstly, an introduction to Maslow's hierarchy of needs. (Diagram below). It is important for you to understand how you fit into this system, now that the rug has been pulled out from under your feet.

Read this from the bottom up.

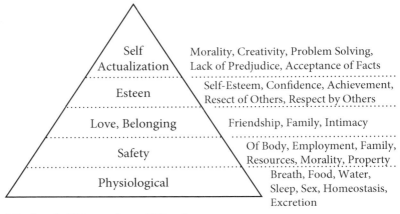

Maslow's Hierarchy of Needs

1. Physiological: Do you have enough money for food, your rent/mortgage, are you drinking enough water, are you getting enough sleep and exercise, are you warm and comfortable? Write down a few things that you are happy with and a few that you need to work on now.

2. Safety: This is not just a physical safety aspect. It goes a bit further—are you able to earn money, is your property secure, are your bills being paid, do you have a plan for your future? Importantly, you do feel safe at home and the places you go to?

3. Love and Belonging: There may be a huge gap in this part of your life right now, but you know that you were loved and have still have friends and family around. You may join a group of like-minded people so that you do not feel complete

aloneness. Your emotions are also included in this category of needs—and they could be a point of discomfort and feeling that you don't know how to move forward. You have to believe that you can. The choice is yours—but you will need to do some reaching out. Write here what groups you would like to join.

4. Esteem: This is when you re-discover yourself, your strengths and how you see yourself moving forward. How happy are you now, what makes you happy and how do you feel about yourself? Write a few sentences here about your perception of your confidence now.

5. Self-actualisation: This is about arriving at a place in your life when you know who you are and what you want to be. You now start thinking outside the box, learning, making decisions, become aware of your values and beliefs. Moreover, finding fulfilment in helping others takes on a complete new meaning. Are you happy with you, do you trust yourself, do you want to spend time in your own company?

Because of your loss, the shock that has reverberated though your life and unsettled your habits and flow of life, has thrown you a curve-ball—you may feel disjointed, upside down, not know who you are, where you are going or what you want in your life right now. That's OK!

You may perceive that this confusion has set you back a bit, but it is really just another step in dealing with the fact that you've lost a large part of your life. Sit up, be mindful and patient with yourself, take stock and give yourself a bit of time to heal.

There is light at the end of the tunnel. Without warning, though, you will find that you're having a breakthrough and can move forward.

Do This:

In the meantime, do not panic—stay in the process of healing by doing the 'exercises' in this book to get you to a place where you know that you are healing.

You know what your strengths are.

Write 5 of them here to reinforce that you can get through this time:

1. _____

2. _____

3. _____

4. _____

5. _____

Look at them carefully

Which of these have you neglected recently?

Circle the most important one in a colour that you like—this is about being yourself again…

- Decide what you want to do about it in the next hour

  _____.

- Write down exactly what action to take—be creative, think outside the box. Be clear about the details!)

  _____.

- Now transfer what you have written onto a Post-It note and put it where you can see it.

- Put this book down right now and go and do exactly what you said you want to do.

- Once it's done…put a large tick and write DONE across it. Then pat yourself on the back.

- How do you feel now?

  _____.

Use this list whenever you feel fragile or low.

To learn more, visit: www.yournewbeginningbook.com

Addiction

Addiction is not just about drugs, alcohol, gambling or smoking. You may think that you do not need to read this, but I'm going to address a different addiction.

Are you addicted to suffering?

This is THE most important acknowledgement that you can make to yourself—Yes or No? Think about it seriously. Be honest with yourself.

Do you 'suffer in silence', do you need to talk about suffering all the time, do you experience this in many facets of your life?

Have you been brought up to believe that you need to suffer? Many religious beliefs tell you this. Really? Do you really think that a God of love would want you to suffer? If your subconscious is telling you that you have to suffer, why do you think it is? Write it here _____

_____

This is a behaviour adopted by many people who have lost somebody or something big in their life.

Can you remember when you were still quite small and you liked to play in a mud puddle.

At first you would dig a place for a hole. Then, when the ground was stirred up a bit, you would go and fetch water— sometimes in a cup or maybe a watering can—just enough to get it started. You would stir it with a stick until it became a small area of mud in a hole. Then you'd run to the tap, get more water, stir it in and get excited—running between your water source and stirring.

Eventually you would put your hands into the mud and let it ooze through your fingers. This would boost your excitement and you would make it bigger—just a lump at a time. Then you would stand in it and screech in glee as the sloppy mud oozed between your toes. Your delight was taken even further when you decided that you wanted to sit in it. Heaven!

Yes—you became addicted to making your mud-bath. Today people would pay you lots of money to wallow in it!

Your addiction to this, though, was short-lived. I got into big trouble for my biggest mud-bath ever. So—my young first addiction of squishy, squelchy mud came to an abrupt end when I got into huge trouble (I won't bore you with the painful details of my posterior for a few days). That stopped me from making another one—forever. Today, I have no desire to do ANY activity where I have to insert my body into the mud.

WHAT IF . . .

What if my mother had told me that I could play in my mud-bath all day? Every day. What if all my friends joined me and I was the centre of the group—and they all had to bring more water, stir it and bring soil from the garden to make it even bigger? What if I could roll in it and watch all my on-lookers squealing in delight? What if some of them were allowed to join me—sometimes—or maybe, all we would want was roll in this mud-bath? What if my mother told me all the benefits of mud and how it is excellent for your skin and that this is what you should be doing to keep that tender beautiful young-looking face? Wow! I would even want to sleep in it, and even think of eating it!

Ok, so what does this mud-bath experience have to do with your addiction to suffering?

Well, if you sit in one place in your mud-bath all the time, it becomes deeper and deeper, and you could eventually stand in it up to your knees—I had one like that. You could quite easily be so impressed that it becomes a habit, and you would want to do it all the time. Eventually you would need to have that mud-bath or your day would feel incomplete—something missing.

I'm not going to beat around the bush here—'Suffering' can so easily become a habit. With people admiring and edging you on to suffer more—recalling all you painful experiences, talking them over and over, stirring the mud for and with you; feeling sorry for you and bringing more water to make sure it doesn't dry out—keeping the emotions raw and fresh and moist—this creates an addiction to suffering.

Do you, like a 'friend' I had before, want to keep yourself 'addicted to your suffering?' (Maybe a visit to the AA will open your eyes—they may try to help you.)

You have to trust yourself enough and want to get out of this addiction to negativity, self-destruction and feeling sorry for yourself. (I'm not going to apologise. This is up to you. You can do it if you want to be happy.)

Trust Yourself

When I was about 12 years old, we moved to a new city. We had always moved around from place to place because of my dad's work. This was nothing new. One skill I had learned by this age, was how to pack glasses into boxes, wrapped in such a way that they would arrive safely on the other side, even with rough handling by the movers.

We always took the photo albums, along with our really valuable things, in the car with us. This particular move, my mother insisted very forcibly that we would not do this. It was a long journey and she said the car would be too full—everything had to go into the removal truck. Everything, except what we needed for the one overnight stay.

I secretly packed most of my favourite childhood belongings—very important parts of my life—into a special bag and stashed it right into the back of the boot of the car. I had a nagging, uneasy feeling in my stomach about sending it in the truck. OMG! My mother found it before the truck left, took it out, shoved it into a box that still had some space in it. That was it! There was absolutely NO CHOICE! It had to go in the truck.

We arrived at our new house early the next morning, having stayed over en-route at a cheap little motel. Our new house was big, had a lovely garden, was near shops, the library and not too far from my new school. We walked through the rooms, deciding how we were going to arrange our furniture, who would be sleeping where and we met our new neighbours.

At 11 o'clock we were waiting in the garden, looking down the road, each trying to be the first to see the blue 'King's Transport' truck. It didn't arrive at 11. So we waited patiently. And we waited. And we waited. And we waited.

No blue 'King's Transport' truck. And still we waited.

This was before mobile phones were around, so my dad would walk across the street to a payphone and call the

'King's Transport' office. No answer! He called every hour, then more often . . . still no answer. We were all starting to get worried. I was thinking about my precious belongings that my mother had taken from the car—I had a sinking feeling inside as the day dragged on.

Eventually I had to go to the shops to get take-aways—we couldn't all go in case they arrived. That awful feeling in my stomach grew worse—I couldn't eat. Still nothing. By 6pm there was no sign of the truck, and it was getting dark.

We waited until very late, but still nothing arrived. We decided to leave a large note on the front door, saying that we would be there at the first light in the morning. We also gave the hotel number to the neighbours—just in case they arrived at some silly hour in the night.

We were there before 6 the next morning—bright and early, ready to receive our things! Still no truck! Nothing! More calls from the public callbox, still no answer. Then . . . at about lunch time, they answered the phone!

My Dad asked them when we could expect our things and what was going on. The guy on the other side of the phone said: "Mr V, did you not read your paper this morning?" My dad tried to be polite: "Well, if I had my couch to sit on, maybe I would have, but why are you asking me that?"

The story was on the front page of the paper! He said that the driver, after leaving the original city, had pulled over on the side of the road in the evening to get some sleep. As he had turned the large, heavy truck off the road in the middle of the desert, he had not realised how deep the camber was at that exact spot—I think he may have been half asleep—and the truck fell over onto its side next to the road.

He had radioed to the office for help. They had gathered all the staff at the depot, collected the equipment they needed, and had driven the five hours to the scene—about 500km away—to see what could be done. That's why there was no answer at the office.

Apparently, when they got there, they decided to weld brackets onto the bottom and sides of the truck in an attempt to lift it back onto its wheels. (No comment on this idea—blankets wrapped for protection around the furniture, cardboard boxes, etc . . . say no more!)

Well, within seconds of starting the welding, they had to run for their lives—they had just lit the biggest bonfire in the desert—maybe it was even visible from space.

We had lost everything! It had all gone up in smoke! Everything that was special to me—my medals, awards, childhood photographs, books, my art, everything gone in one big bonfire—and I wasn't there to roast a marshmallow or enjoy the fireworks that I'm sure went with it.

Wow! That was huge. (I've never, ever put any of my precious items into a removal truck again.) As a teenager, to deal with this kind of loss was enormous for me. I was angry, really angry. I was frustrated, had lost what I then felt was the evidence of who I was. I had to let those emotions go.

I submerged myself into writing poetry, starting a new life with nothing to show for my experiences until then. It was hard, my parents also found it really difficult (I can understand that more now as an adult) . . . however, I was told to just get over it.

This was a turning point in my life. I knew that my gut instincts were right and that I could trust who I was. I was learning that I had to take control of my life and that I wanted to start being who I really was. Ok, I was a teenager; with imminent changes . . . however, the shock of this event did make me think more about whom and what I wanted to be, and stand up for what I wanted.

In a strange way, this had left an empty space inside me, a re-look at how I was just doing what I was told to do, and I could do NOTHING to get back any of my things. I could only look forward.

Believe me, there were many tears, many regrets, much blame, many angry and ranting outbursts, sad, emotional moments—but I had to work through it and get on with life. I had to deal with the loss and accept this fact, try to find a lesson that I could learn from it and not dwell on the negative.

I couldn't sit in a mud-hole and feel sorry for myself. I had to trust myself enough to get on with a brand new life.

Have you had any other time in your life when you lost something or someone special—something big?

How did you feel then? What did you do to get yourself through that time? You have done it—even though your previous losses may have been much smaller, but each of these was still quite significant in your life.

Do This:

Write how you felt and what you did to deal with the situation.

You are older now, have learned more lessons and have greater insight into how to cope. Looking back, remind yourself of some of the lessons you learned about dealing with what happened then, and bring some of that into your consciousness to help you now.

Let yourself know that you accept yourself, know that you can stick with the process and persist in finding your way through this time in your life.

_____

_____

_____

_____

Trust yourself totally. You may wonder how you can do this when the little voices from your subconscious are telling you that you can't be trusted.

Trust your 'gut feelings'. Trust your desires. Trust your knowledge of who you really are, what you really are and what you want in your life. If people tell you not to make any decisions soon after you have experienced this big loss, trust yourself to know when you are ready. Trust that you will make the right decisions and trust that you will be OK. Trust your relationship with yourself, what you want for your future, your relationships with others, your actions and belief in yourself—just trust them all. Just Do It!

Below, make a list of all the areas you still need to learn to trust, and then know that you can make it happen.

_____

_____

_____

_____

Trust yourself so that you can 'become what you might be'.

Intention vs. Motion

The road to hell is paved with good intentions. You know this saying. So what does your road look like?

By now, you are looking at your life, who and what you are and what you want in your life from now. You know that you have to get your act together at some time to move forward, in spite of this event which crossed your path.

Do This:

As I've suggested so many times, writing changes your energy and releases stress. Just write or draw pictures if you want—even just writing words will work.

Write down things that you have been intending to do—go back as far as you can—things you wanted to do but didn't get around to. Things you know you 'should' do that are on your list. Things that you have wished and dreamed about—Write them all here.

_____   _____

_____   _____

_____   _____

_____   _____

_____   _____

_____   _____

Decide which two of those you want to put onto a different list—the list of new habits you want to store in your subconscious. (Don't do too many—even one is OK to start). Write one in each box below

Transfer these onto Post-It notes with the date you want to start—today is good!

Getting back to your subconscious: It will tell you that there is no way in hell that you can do what you've just written on the Post-Its. It will shout at you and try to convince you that you need to give up before starting. It may concede on a few things and you may have to accept a few of these demands too. (If you wanted to be a gymnast when you were 4 years old, admit the reality—it's much too late in your life and physically not possible to compete in the Olympics now.)

However, you could find a creative way to do something for yourself along those lines. Take up yoga or Pilates or a form of 'gymnastic style' exercise You could even invent your own to do at home or wherever you exercise—in the pool, the gym, the park—go for it!

A gentle reminder . . . If you stay sitting in your mud-puddle, you will stay there. If you just sit there, nothing new will happen in your life. You will not heal or grow.

Get out of that puddle—move—just one small step at a time—and then keep moving—like that little blue engine. You will gain momentum and your path will no longer be paved with good intentions. Only you can make this difference in your life.

Get Out of Your Own Way

GET OUT OF YOUR OWN WAY! Yes! You heard me correctly.

Get out of your own way!

Really—what does that mean? If you think I'm being a bit harsh, we all get in our own way much of the time. Take your time to come to terms and accept that you can be OK. However, some of your beliefs, perceptions and habits will have to change for you to change, adapt, deal with and heal from this unpleasant experience.

You are doing well so far and will continue until the scars are only reminders of the good times. If you are still 'reeling with shock and anxiety' often, just acknowledge that now you are aware of this part of the process when losing a loved one.

If you are still feeling the impact of the loss which results in:

Sadness
Frustration
Helplessness
Self-doubt
Grief
Mixed feelings
Loneliness

and many more—all playing havoc within you -

- then it is time to sit down and have a talk with yourself.

If you are really struggling, you may be too focused on the negative blow that this had on your life. This is why you need to 'get out of your own way'.

What does this mean?

It means that you need to stop thinking too much and stop over-analysing things that happen in your life. Stop trying to be who others think you are. Stop trying to be brave:

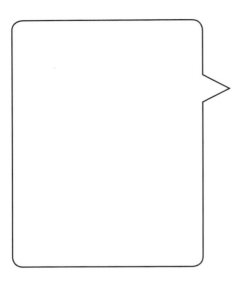

Allow yourself to feel, to be and allow your life to flow in the direction that you want it to go.

How can you do this?

Another unconventional way to 'get out of your own way is to do the exercise below:

1. Draw a picture of yourself in the box above.

2. Set your alarm for about 20 minutes. Sit quietly and be aware of where you are in your life <u>right now,</u> observe all the above-mentioned feelings, thoughts and perceptions and write words around your picture.

3. Re-look at your picture to write your answers:

    1. What lesson can I learn from this whole experience so far?

        _____

    2. How committed am I to getting to a place in my life where I am OK?

        _____

3. What are my strengths that I can rely on to get through this?

_____

4. What do I believe about my healing process?

_____

5. My intention is to be strong, mindful, aware, and know that I am healing and that I will be OK!

Signed: _____ Date: _____

Do This:

NOW—go and do something creative—sing, dance, play/listen to music, go for a walk, look for small things on the pathway.

Play a kids game with yourself, skip along the path, close your eyes and pretend that you are a ____ (whatever makes you feel happy, excited about life and be like a kid without limitations).

If there was a time of illness through which you were supporting your loved one, please understand that this 'emotional support' also had an impact on you—and now the routine has changed.

You had such strength during this time. While the habit of caring will have left a chasm of emptiness that you have to deal with on top of the loss, your attention was mostly on the other person. How often did people ask you how you were? Your strength of character got you through this period. Use it now to move your life forward in a positive direction.

Even though some people were concerned and interested in your well-being at the time, most of them were focused on the one going through the mental, physical, emotional tension, insecurities and fears.

Even though you are a really strong person, it DID affect you—your subconscious knows and will remind you—no matter how long it's been.

Do This: Don't leave yourself to hope that 'time will heal'. This person would not have wanted you to be sad and hurt forever! They would want you to love and celebrate the happy times you had and find peace and joy in your life again. This cannot happen if you are very focused on being sad, miserable and needing pity.

It is time to release the impact of this event in your life. Hold onto the great memories and start re-building your life.

I, _____ acknowledge and know that this time in my life was for me to learn a lesson, and now I choose:

- to accept that I have a lesson to learn from it,
- to work through this process and commit to healing myself.

Signed: _____ Date: _____

Now . . .

Now that you have begun to realise what you have behind you, in the present and in front of you—it is time to 'get out of your own way'.

If you think I'm a bit crazy—that's fine. How is it possible to get out of your own way?

Let's look at your 'shadow self'. If you are not sure what that is—go and stand in the sun and look for your shadow. That is a reflection of you.

It is also that other part of you running your life—your subconscious mind. You are fully aware too now, that your experiences in life cannot be changed or erased.

The good news is: There is a way to get out of your own way.

The past is past—it's history—over, finished done. It cannot repeat itself. By doing the same things you did in the past, you feel, expect and get the same results.

Little by little you can start taking action to change the things you don't want hanging around—'cos they make you feel yuk and you want to feel great!

Do This:

Every morning, set yourself an 'intention' for the day—even before you jump out of bed (as you do! Ha-Ha!). Decide what you intend to do, think, feel and be.

Make it a habit—it doesn't happen overnight—but each and every little step you take will make a difference.

Get out of your own way, decide to step out of your little box and keep moving slowly in the direction you want.

Go to your garden and watch a snail. It keeps moving in one direction . . . over obstacles, through furrows and keeps going till it finds a place where it wants to stop under a leaf. Learn from it.

Make a list of habits or thoughts that you know get in your way of success, being you and dealing with this loss.

Get your colours and number them in order of how much they stop you.

When you pull these out of your subconscious mind—be aware that they have very long roots—some are deeply embedded into your psyche / being. Be patient with yourself. Do this with the utmost of care for yourself. Love yourself, honour yourself and respect yourself. Remember that it is a process—stick with it and watch the results.

Using the same colours as in the box, write what you want to do about these habits / thoughts that get in your way:

1. _____

2. _____

3. _____

4. _____

Like weeds growing in the middle of a beautiful flower bed, right next to the plants you want to keep, these old habits and ways of living that don't work for you have to be pulled out carefully, one by one, roots and all, and thrown away.

Get them out of the way, and you will realise that you are getting out of your own way.

To learn more, visit: www.yournewbeginningbook.com

7

Lift Yourself Up

Don't be timid and squeamish about your actions. All life is an experiment. The more experiments you make the better.

—Ralph Waldo Emerson.

Understand Your Self, Your Journey

T O UNDERSTAND YOURSELF better, get out of your own way. You have to look at yourself from how others see you. No, not comparing yourself or asking their opinion—this can best be achieved by playing a game with yourself.

Do This:

Imagine that you are a fly on the wall.

You are looking down on three conversations **you** are having: one with a friend, one with a family member, and one with a work colleague.

You, the fly, are here to observe without prejudice or judgements—the words, emotions and perceptions of the two people chatting.

Conversation 1:

You: _____

Friend: _____

You: _____

Friend: _____

You: _____

Friend: _____

You: _____

Friend: _____

You: _____

Friend: _____

Conversation 2:

You: _____

Family member: _____

You: _____

Family member: _____

You: _____

Family member: _____

You: _____

Family member: _____

You:_____

Family member:_____

Conversation 3:

You:_____

Colleague: _____

You:_____

Colleague: _____

You:_____

Colleague: _____

You:_____

Colleague: _____

You:_____

Colleague: _____

What have you learned about yourself? What are your fears?
What are your beliefs? From this different perspective, what
have you noticed about you?

_____

_____

_____

_____

_____

_____

Take stock of the lessons you have learned in your life. You have to forge a way through your thoughts, feelings and facts about yourself, to finding a path where you are happy and how you envisage yourself.

Not in the mud puddle, but the path on which you are moving forward, one step at a time.

Here are some questions to help you on your journey:

What really matters to you?	
What do you still need to understand about yourself and your life?	
What one question do you have that you cannot answer?	
What is your purpose in life? (Or why are you here?)	
What is one thing that you are passionate about?	

How big or small are you compared to others around you?	
What are your biggest self-doubts?	
What one thing really stands out to you in your life that is 'standing in your way' right now?	
What one thing do you really understand about yourself?	
Looking back over your life, what do you feel has left a negative impact on you?	
What is the best thing you learned that you are using in your life right now?	

Where can you find peace? Is it already in your life—or is it outside? Or is it hiding?	
Are you happy with your own company? Just you? Comment!	

Having answered these questions, acknowledge that you have taken a long step forward in getting to know yourself better.

How are you feeling now? _____

Congratulate yourself on taking this step. Unlocking who you are is vital for you, not to just heal, but to embrace the change, the loss and allow yourself to be OK during this time of dealing with what's happened.

I find this saying by Knott Gregson very empowering. Write it on a Post-It and stick it where you can read it every day:

"Say it to yourself, over and again, until its echo becomes the lullaby that lulls you to sleep, the chimes that wake you:

There is nothing I cannot do,

There is no one I cannot be.

Of this fact, You, have always been the only one that needs convincing".

Your Platform

You are creating a platform from which you operate—a place to which you can come back to if you get lost, a place where you can stay for a while, to rest, and a place high enough for you to look around and make choices and decisions. From here you can take the next step forward to your new beginning.

Now that you're on this 'stage', you can create the necessary strategies and plans that will lead you in the direction you have chosen. These tools are your habits, values, beliefs, perceptions, mindfulness, your attributes and talents.

Nobody is promising you a smooth ride. It may be bumpy, but if you trust yourself enough—accepting that you have what you need for your journey—you can still learn and gain more inspiration or epiphanies along the way.

You know you can do this and that you'll come out stronger. Let's create a 'tool' to assist you when your 'thoughts & perceptions' need some attention.

Do This:

Create your own toolbox of mind-empowering 'characteristics', readily available and at your service, whenever you need them.

Set your timer for 20 minutes and fill in Part 1 and Part 2.

Part 1

Here is a list to start you thinking about some of your strengths, your positive personality traits and attributes you have used to get through some tough times in your life. Pull these out of the dusty cupboard of your subconscious and dust them off:

Determination, courage, persistence, patience, an open mind, passion for life, resilience, mind-power.

Add you own here:

Part 2

The next step is to look at what your subconscious may be feeding your mind. Thoughts and perceptions that drain you and negate your good attributes:

Indecision, fear, apathy, self-doubt, inflexibility, confusion, permission, grounding.

Add you own here:

Part 3

Classify your self-talk 'thoughts & perceptions' into whether they 'drain' you or whether you 'gain' some sense of positivity, energy and joy from them. This is a great reference from which you can extract exactly what you need at any given point in time, place and situation.

These DRAIN me . . .	I GAIN . . . from these . . .

Familiarise yourself with all your positive attributes. Memorise them. Write them on Post-Its and repeat them to yourself at least three times a day. They will be there for you immediately when you need them.

How will you find space in your life to add in more habits and new ways to cope?

Out with the Old—In with the New

When you do food shopping and you arrive home with bags of exciting, fresh food, you have to empty out quite a few of the old things in your fridge to make space for the new.

Ask Gordon Ramsey! If you do not throw that old food out first, it will definitely contaminate the fresh food.

Similarly, if you are buying a new car, you may need to get rid of the old one to create space in the garage. Or if you are purchasing extra clothes, the old ones go to a 'charity shop'. There's no space for the new ones until the old ones are out of the way.

Well, life's exactly like that too. And it is time for you now to make space for the new. No, it will not happen overnight, but you must be mindful and aware that this is a vital step forward. The good news is that you decide the size of each new step forward, and how many you will take at a time.

[A quick word about starting a 'new' relationship (if you lost your partner). This is not what I mean by 'out with the old, in with the new'. You have to give yourself enough time to heal. Ensure you are comfortable with your own company and in your own space. You have to be OK and settled on your own. Simply learn to trust, believe in and spend time with yourself first.]

You do NOT want this to boomerang on you—listen to yourself, be happy with yourself and ensure that you are fully aware that your loved one cannot be replaced.

A person I know, quite soon after the passing of her husband, fell head over heels in love and completely infatuated with a work colleague. He was flattered, showed some interest in all the attention, but it was never in his plan to be involved with her. Years later, it was still just that—her obsession, his enjoyment of the attention and company—but not the relationship that she yearned for. Often she would wonder why nothing was moving forward in their 'relationship', but it was completely one-sided.

Somebody else I know pursued a new partnership soon after his wife had passed on. They got married and then the problems started—because he had not found himself first, he was expecting this new lady to replace his wife—but she was a very different person. He started harassing her and getting really upset and annoyed at her for not doing things the same way his late wife had done. He just could not let go and became more determined to change her. Sadly, it didn't work and, when she opted out of her 'hell-hole'—he ended up having to cope with a huge loss all over again.

Rebound is more likely to hurt you rather than fulfil you or bring happiness. You have to first be happy with yourself and then that empty space in your life can be filled.

Get onto that platform you created, get out of your own way, look at yourself from a different point of view and decide which 'old' habits, thoughts and feelings you want to throw out. Decide what you want for yourself—have a *clear, detailed* picture in your mind before doing anything bold.

As soon as you start getting rid of an old habit, you need to start replacing it with the new. Be patient with yourself—

remember the process has to take time to settle into your subconscious—it will NOT happen overnight or in 'the twinkling of an eye'.

Choose what you want to teach your subconscious mind; imagine how much you will enjoy the new routine; decide exactly what colours you will paint your walls; make a commitment to when you will practice your new hobby and establish what you will say to yourself when you look in the mirror.

You're doing this already—this is a gentle reminder.

Small Steps: The Way Forward

As you know, Rome wasn't built in a day. This saying reminds us that life is made up of a variety of features—experiences, beliefs, perceptions and thoughts are all part of your make-up. Even though each, on its own, is a small aspect of your life, they are all like bricks—every one a vital part of a wall; a piece of a puzzle—If one is missing or damaged, the whole picture is spoiled.

As recommended, do not just jump into making a decision if you are not able to think rationally.

Everybody kept telling me that I should not make major decisions about anything for at least six months to a year or longer after my husband had died. Yes—I knew this and was going to follow this advice carefully—after all, this was a first for me and I had no idea how it was going to pan out, let alone what my life would be like six months or two years from then.

Wow! Did I not hear this or what? I went on a holiday to get away and try to find myself. Obviously 'myself' had run away to another country, and then it just so happened that I 'just' bought a property. It was cheap, but somehow it spoke to me and said that it had been waiting for me for a long time and that this was the place that had been in the back of my mind for years.

I had found that space. It just happened to be there and everything around it fell into place. Somehow I knew that this was not a step but a massive jump forward. I had thirty days to decide. Was this right for me, or was I jumping on the 'bandwagon' at a whim? Would it turn out to be the best decision during this time of uncertainty and confusion? Or would I regret it later? Until now, I thought I hadn't yet found myself or what I wanted in life . . . and now this.

Looking back, it was a dream that I'd had for years. I discussed it with my son soon after my initial crazy offer to buy it. He remembered that, when he was quite young, I would tell him, that one day I would have a property close to the sea, where people could come for retreats and get away from the rat-race to re-fresh and find themselves.

I'm not advocating you do this—but I was just at the right place at the right time and had the means to get my dream started.

And somehow, it just brought me, with a big bump, to a place where I knew I had to find myself and start living my dream—I felt really good about my find! (Just DID it!)

Was I lucky, or was this just part of my healing and re-discovery of myself? I believe my long-term vision of what I wanted, helped me see who I am and learn to trust myself. It just found me when I was at a low place, cheered me up and helped me on my way.

Start storing new thoughts, feelings, ideas, perceptions and beliefs step-by-step in your cupboard of experiences. It will pay off when you most need it—just like it happened to me.

Because I had been doing this for a while in my life, when the right opportunity fell into my lap, all the inner work I'd been doing on myself paid off. My dream peeked at me and said: 'Boo! I'm here! Now you have to make it work!"

Familiarise yourself with the basic steps as set out below, and when they come along and pop onto your path, you will know what you're dealing with and can be more prepared.

Even though this may not be completely unconventional, the essence is about you knowing that you will be guided into taking small steps—one at a time.

My shock into reality didn't necessarily happen in this order, but I had already stored these into my subconscious, so it worked for me, not against me.

No matter if you are only starting this process now, it will start working for you immediately. Keeping at it will bring your new ideas to life.

Get yourself prepared starting now.

Five steps to healing:

1. Acknowledge your BS.

2. Be clear about what you want.

3. Create a new habit.

4. Decide & commit.

5. Energise yourself and Just Do It.

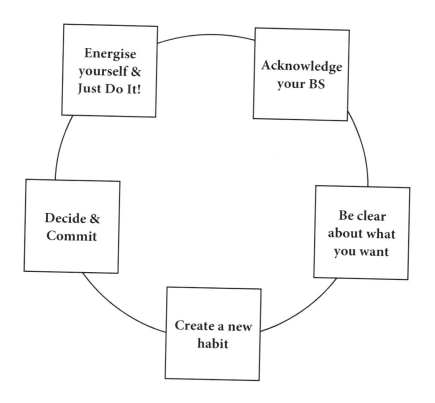

To learn more, visit: www.yournewbeginningbook.com

Daily 'Exercises' to Lift Yourself

I'm not suggesting that you rush off to the gym for a few hours of working out every day. The exercises I'm referring to, are the ones that influence your emotional, mental, creative and spiritual balance. The physical elements are equally as important, so I'll start with those.

The physical component, your body, has to be ok—this is you. All the other aspects of you need a healthy body to be able to operate effectively—or at all. So, firstly focus on keeping your body in good condition.

1. Water: Ensure that you are drinking enough water—around 8 glasses a day. This will help not only your body but also your mind to function at it's best.

2. Sleep: It is very important to get enough sleep. Listen to your body and sleep when you need to. Your body restores itself during sleep.

3. Rest: A time when you are awake, but taking note of your thoughts and enjoying just being where you are—lying in a warm bath; feet up with a cup of hot chocolate; just really minding your own business in a calm, tranquil, quiet way. This is a vital time to getting to know who you are, who you want to be and dream in silence for a while. Take this me-time seriously.

4. Relaxation: It is important to take some time out for yourself to be quiet and just relax your mind, do some form of meditation or spoil yourself with some 'me-time'.

5. Exercise: Get some exercise. If you do not usually exercise—get out there and just start walking a bit—it will re-energise you. In the beginning you may feel a bit tired but after a few times you will start feeling the benefits.

6. Diet: It is really important to ensure that you get your fresh foods and a balanced diet. Stay away from sugar and too many refined food. If you overeat too many unhealthy foods, you will start to feel sluggish, not good about yourself and could struggle to find mental clarity. Watch out for binge-eating spells, or the opposite.

There are many creative ways that you can treat yourself to making a difference in your life:

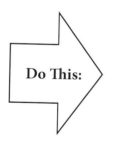

Do This:

- Get fresh flowers for a special place in your house.
- Get a few different coloured coffee mugs and choose a different one every day.
- Have a bubble bath, light some candles and play some music and relax.
- Wear a different colour outfit just to be daring.
- Get some very bright Post-It notes and write reminders to yourself, sticking them up in unusual places around your home.
- Try a different flavour of herbal tea.
- Get a colouring book and do some colouring.

- Eat different colour-of-the-rainbow foods—a different one each day.
- Doodle with a pen on a small piece of paper for 10 minutes.
- Watch something funny on u-tube and have a good laugh.
- Talk to yourself in the mirror.
- Get coloured gel pens and write with them instead of just black or blue.
- Listen to your intuition.
- Get a really bright different colour nail varnish—shock yourself.

Just do it and enjoy!

To learn more, visit: www.yournewbeginningbook.com

Create Your Ideal Day

One way that you can take a small step which could feel like a leap, is to create your ideal day. It takes a bit of thinking and looking at yourself from a different angle again. I did this years ago and it is starting to happen for me now.

Imagine that you have no limits—you have just won a competition where you can create your best day—not a holiday—a normal working day.

What will you do—when will you get up; what will you do before breakfast; describe you breakfast table; who will you meet; what will you have for lunch; where will you spend the afternoon; what will your home or office look like; when will you have an evening meal and what will that be; what will you do after your meal; how will you spend the evening and with whom; finally, what will your room look like, and what will you do just before dropping off to sleep?

Dream, imagine, think what you really would like your day to be like, describe it in detail so you can read, re-read again and again. Write your dream day below:

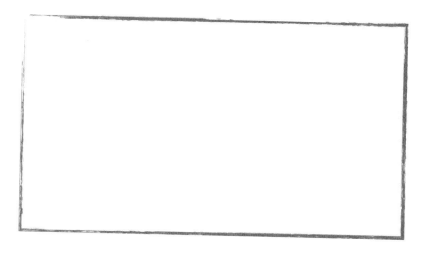

You'll feel good once you have this as a vision of your life—even if it does not all come to fruition—just thinking about it—that clear picture—makes a difference. I've sometimes just gone out with my picture in mind and had a great day. Enjoy creating it!

This is a small step, but with your senses added, you can make it big—keep it as your dream—make it alive. There will be times when you imagine that this is your lifestyle and you may recognise, realise and create some small details into your life starting now.

Something that I wanted to have as a part of my ideal day was to go to the gym for just a short while every morning—to get the blood flowing, the muscles agile, breathing deeply and feeling light and proud that I'm going regularly. Well, I joined a gym on a special promotion—so got it at a good price—and go every morning—5 days a week. I wanted that, and I'm doing it . . . I'm not bragging or trying to make you look bad because you aren't going the gym, but that is what I wanted. And I've got that part of my ideal daydream. A few other things have also started falling into place.

It's because I wrote it down, imagined what it would be like. I kept that picture alive, active, clear and fresh in my thoughts.

It's fun—just do it!

To learn more, visit: www.yournewbeginningbook.com

8

It's Not Your Fault
[Healing from Suicide]

Forgive yourself for not having the foresight to know what now seems so obvious in hindsight.
—Judy Belmont

Hearing the News

WHEN YOU WERE told the news, it was perhaps the most devastating moment you have ever experienced. The shock, overwhelming emotions and your reactions need to be wrapped in a soft ambience of care for yourself—even now. Decide to recall these slowly, with gentleness and mindfulness. Be aware that to start the healing process, a tender approach will bring you closer to finding a way to dealing with this awful event.

Do This: Get yourself a pen and blank-page notebook that you can use as a journal—small enough to fit into your bag or pocket. Once you have these, you are ready to start this process. Keep it close so you can write whenever you need to.

Find a place where you feel safe without interruptions.

When you are ready to start, close your eyes for a few minutes and just bring yourself into the present moment.

Bring your loved one into your presence and imagine that he or she is standing in front of you.

Notice your emotions, your thoughts and the physical sensations in your body. When you are ready, take a deep breath, open your eyes and write a few words, phrases, sentences describing what you are feeling. Write in the present tense to access this event fully. Write until you are empty.

Close your eyes again and observe your inner qualities that you would like to bring into this moment to help you cope with the pain, the shock and the trauma linked to this event—your compassion, understanding, care, empathy and your perspective.

Write these into your journal using a different colour.

Now bring yourself back to the present. Recognise these positive 'tools' that you can use to work through these emotions.

What was your first reaction? Horror, disbelief, un-nerving, inconceivable, chilled . . . questions, questions, questions . . . no answers?

Because the news of a person close to you taking their own life is completely unexpected and untimely, the shock is devastating and intimidating, to say the least. If somebody was ill or even died in an accident, the action causing death is different. Suicide leaves the greatest, most significant, unanswered question of all: WHY? This time, there are no answers.

Automatically your subconscious will kick in, with you blaming yourself for not seeing the signs, for not being there for them, for having that last argument with them, for not doing more, for neglecting your duty, for . . .

Immediately after this incident, you were reeling in disbelief and confusion. You may be living with this agonising event still hanging over you. This is normal. Now that you are reading this book, you can, even long after it has happened, start working through the pain and the even larger crushing effect that this had on you.

People will all say to you: 'It's not your fault', but that doesn't help at all—easier said than done.

Let's find some ways to work through this . . .

Acknowledge

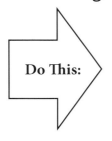

Do This:

Firstly, please give yourself permission to heal and acknowledge this tragic event in your life.

Close your eyes for a few minutes while sitting quietly and tell yourself:

'I give myself permission and acknowledge that I have not understood the reasoning for _____ to take their own life.'

'I allow myself to take part in my own healing.'

Have you acknowledged that this person made a decision to end their life here on earth? This is the first vital step that you *must* take to heal. If you omit recognising that it was *their* choice, you will always carry the burden of what they did, without finding peace.

Even if you feel you have, write it here:

Do This:

I acknowledge that _____ came to a place in his / her life, that they felt it was better to end life here on earth.

Write this onto a Post-It note and keep it in a place where you can see it regularly. Read it to yourself at least 5 times a day— every day without fail.

You have to communicate this clearly to your caring, inner subconscious mind. It will *slowly* begin to understand that you are not to blame for their decision.

Acceptance vs. Blame

You will be trying really hard to understand what happened. I have some bad news. It is very unlikely that you will ever really understand fully why they made this decision and took this action. You may feel that it is important for you to know, however, they are no longer here to talk to.

Understanding their thoughts, their feelings, and their perceptions is what was in their head. There will be unspoken ideas, fears, failings, discouragement, pain, and disappointment (to name but a few) that they never expressed—all inside their subconscious mind that led them to this act.

For you to spend hours mulling over how you could have changed that, well, sadly it is too late. This special person had something inside that caused such discomfort to them, that they could no longer bear it.

Please do not allow yourself to be drawn into their despondency. It is time for you to accept their decision, no matter how you may miss them or feel that they have abandoned or betrayed you, or that you could have changed their life for them.

The distressing fact is that they had to take responsibility for their own life, and this is how they felt they needed to deal with life. For them, they felt that it was their only option at that time. Life had become too difficult to deal with. The step in doing what they did was a gigantic decision and yes, it has had an enormous impact on you.

So what is the next step?

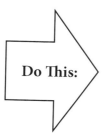

Do This:

- Get your journal and write down all the questions you have for them that are unanswered. Leave quite a bit of space under each one.

- Keep finding more questions until you no longer can think of any.

Once done, use a different colour and write the answers *you* think to each question—from your point of view. Once done, use yet another colour, this time, writing what you think *they* would have said to you when you gave your answer.

Looking at the answers from this different perspective, will help you to acquire a clearer acceptance of their decision. Yes, understanding it will never happen, but by accepting (not condoning) what happened, is an easier way to move on to healing.

Do This:

Take responsibility for your life this minute. Accept the fact that you cannot change what was their life, and that you are in no way responsible for their actions.

You can and need to accept that you are not to blame. Go to a mirror, now and tell yourself this!

The pain and sadness that go with the absence of the person: that you can learn from the other parts of this book.

Here I want to inform you about tools that you can use to create acceptance, rather than blame, which is the only way to healing.

If you think that I'm being hard on you, please do not listen to those little voices. One fact to be aware of, is that the complexity of this person 'opting-out-of-life' has created the need for an intricate process of inner work, for you to come to terms with their actions. You deserve to heal and move on from it.

Most people, who end their lives, do so out of desperation, excessive fears, total confusion and not being able to see a way out of the predicament in which they perceive themselves. They are so anxious about these perceptions that they give up trying, choosing to get sucked into a cavernous mud-hole to the extent that they cannot, or do not to want to, reach out for the help that they so urgently need. Unfortunately, this person is no longer here to learn how to change their life. (Who knows—they may have to come back and re-learn.)

This 'mind-game' of acceptance is something you will need to practice over and over.

You have to accept that they chose to leave. You have to accept that they did not inform you of their decision. Accept that they could see no other way forward. Even if they tried to blame you before the event, accept that their life is their responsibility. Accept that they did or did not blame themselves for their own misery. You have to accept that you may never know the real reason for their decision. Accept that they took responsibility for ending their own life. Accept that you could not stop them this last time.

Please do this mirror acceptance talk as often as you need to tell your subconscious

STOP! It is not your fault!

Make this a priority in your life today.

Go to the mirror, look yourself straight in the eyes and say out loud:

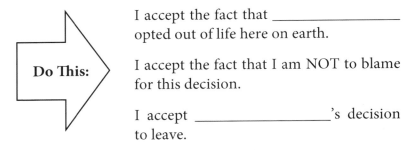

Do This:

I accept the fact that _____ opted out of life here on earth.

I accept the fact that I am NOT to blame for this decision.

I accept _____'s decision to leave.

I accept that I am free from blame and free to heal.

Write this in your journal with the date. Add colour around it and decorate it so that you feel it can bring relief, joy and healing to you. Use lots of green and pink.

Your subconscious will keep reminding you that you feel partly to blame.

I still do this fairly often . . . I look into my mirror and say STOP!

Answer these questions honestly:

1. *How* do you think this person would want you to continue life here?

   _____

2. Do you think that this person was blaming *you* for their decision? (YES/NO)

3. If your answer to no. 2 is yes, write here *what* they said to put this blame onto you _____

   _____

4. How does your answer to no.3 show the *truth*?

   _____

5. If they did *not* blame you, exactly what do you think they would say to you today?

   _____

To learn more, visit: www.yournewbeginningbook.com

The Missing Pieces

Yes, there are an incredible number of missing pieces—The question 'Why?' being the most relevant—even if there was a note.

A very effective way I found, is to write. Not any literary work, not poetry, nothing that will be read by anybody else—just you! Well . . .

Do This:

Get your journal—you may need quite a bit of writing space.

Take some time to think about your dialogue. Imagine that you are going to have a chat with this person—as if they are here.

Write it as a personal dialogue: You and ('x': their name).

Start by having a conversation with this person, about: what you are doing now, what they felt that last day and how they are feeling now. Ask them why they decided to leave.

Ask them what signs you missed. Ask them why they didn't communicate with you about how they were feeling.

During your conversation, ponder for a few moments and imagine that they are telling you what to write. Imagine that you are 'x', answering your questions. Keep up the conversation with them, simply allowing answers to flow into your mind.

The good thing is that, if they are trying to blame you, you can let them know clearly that it is not the truth. Tell them in honesty what you think and how you feel. Tell them what pain they have caused and what effect their decision has had on your life. Say what you want to say. Pretend that they can read this but have to ultimately hear you out.

Be clear, be assertive—if you are angry at them, say it directly. If you become sad, tell them how you feel. If you are afraid to say something, remember that you have the freedom to say anything—they cannot become upset or argue with you. Tell it like it is.

Ask questions about the missing pieces they left behind. Imagine that they are ready to give you answers—the truth.

When you are done, tell them that you forgive them and thank them for giving you some answers.

This journaling exercise can be done as often as you need, whenever you feel the urge and have more to say to them. Next time, start a new page, the date and the next phase of healing.

You will be surprised, if you look back, how you have healed, how your emotions have changed and how your acceptance of their decision will start to become a bit easier. Every time you do this exercise, a part of you will find some healing. I'm still doing journaling when I need to.

Surviving the Attitudes of Others

The Shame of Suicide! I do not know what you believe, or how you feel, but many people feel that it is shameful to have a suicide happen in their family.

If you believe this, you will be hiding it from others, trying to deal with it on your own, healing nowhere in sight.

How do you perceive suicide? _____

If it is your religious belief that suicide is a sin, wrong, and humiliating, how does this relate to you? _____

_____

Considering that you are responsible for your own life, and this person was responsible for theirs, how do you feel this relates to you?

_____

Why do you feel that you cannot tell people what happened?

_____

If you feel that others will blame you, remember that it was a decision that you were not told about. This special person took this unfortunate path of chosing to leave. It is not your fault.

If other people now perceive you in an awkward way because of this—remember that they have their own beliefs, perceptions, thoughts and judgments—and clearly tell this to your subconscious.

Do This:

If you have been around people who feel that you are partly responsible, go to your mirror and do that acceptance talk again.

Please practice this consistently—do not take on their ideas or what they think. After all, if this had happened to them, how would they react and cope? Would it be their fault?

This is where you, by adopting an 'unconventional' way of dealing with this event, know within yourself that your loved one chose this path. You can confidently choose to accept that it was their decision. You can choose to ignore the judgements of others, because you know that it comes from *their* subconscious, *their* perceptions, *their* beliefs and *their* point of view.

Do This:

Kindly tell people that you are aware that your loved one took responsibility for their life and chose this path, even though you do not condone it.

Tell yourself and others (if they hold you responsible), that your loved one is probably happy now, that your bereavement is complex but that you are working through it.

Tell them that they are judging you from their perspective and that you will not be taking that on. If you feel you cannot say it directly to them, write it in your journal—exactly what you'd like to say to them.

Be kind to yourself throughout this time of finding a way to survive your loss. Step back and away from self-judgement. Take the responsibility of informing you subconscious that you are NOT to blame. You are here and have to deal with the loss of your loved one, not the method in which they passed on.

When other people judge you—tell your subconscious mind to ignore their comments; tell your subconscious mind that you know the truth—that your loved one chose the sad path of leaving and that you are dealing with the pain and emptiness only, not the cause.

To learn more, visit: www.yournewbeginningbook.com

Your Belief—Transition

There are many beliefs around what happened, your belief about yourself, your belief about your loved one, your belief about the deed, your belief about where they are now, your belief about your part in this event.

Get your journal again and write your beliefs each in a different colour.

Do This:

1. What I believe about myself is . . .

2. What I believe about this loved one is . . .

3. What I believe about suicide is . . .

4. What I believe about where he or she is now, is . . .

5. What I believe about my part in their decision to die, is . . .

Remember that what you believe has been imprinted in your subconscious mind—since you were born.

The shock of a grim suicide can blast you into disbelief, wondering whether what you perceive life to be is true for you. I've know a number of people who abandon everything they believed in an attempt to deal with the tragic, untimely loss through suicide. Even the word is ignored as you try to avoid the shame that has unfortunately been associated with this decision of ending one's life.

When experiencing any form of trauma, shock or drastic change—change is the common denominator here. If you need to change some of your beliefs, this is perhaps the time to make a decision to look at your life from a different perspective.

Take a strong stance against the beliefs that you have against yourself. If you choose to *ignore* standing your ground in this case, you could end up destroying yourself. However, if you decide to take a path to healing, you can and will be able to cope with the aftermath of this adverse situation.

On a different note: If your loved one wanted to 'punish you' by their decision—stand up for yourself. Do not allow your subconscious to convince you any differently.

Stop! Look at the reality and truth here—they chose their path, allowed their unhappiness to take over and control their perception of how to live. They decided that they wanted out.

Accept this lurid fact and choose life for yourself. Stop kicking against finding a happy ending, allow love to flow into you and heal you—a love for yourself, a love for who you are.

You have to create a transition between taking the blame for somebody else's decision, to embracing the change and adding a positive passion for the gift you still have—life.

To learn more, visit: www.yournewbeginningbook.com

Gaining Perspective

To gain perspective is to stand back and look at all the facts. Be mindful of how you are feeling, of what you believe, and that you are reminding your subconscious mind that you have accepted the fact that your loved one chose to take early leave of their life.

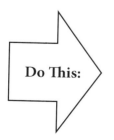

Do This:

Get your journal again and two different colour pens, and continue your healing process:

Imagine that you are sitting on a very high chair—something like the ones they use in tennis competitions.

You are not you, but a neutral onlooker called 'A'. From this perspective, look down at you and your loved one having a conversation—the one just after they have passed. Imagine that you (A) are observing a conversation, to gain some insight and communicate to you—a particular time when these two people were talking.

Sit quietly with your eyes closed and bring yourself into this 'scene'. When you feel that you can detect both standing within earshot of you, take a deep breath, open your eyes and start writing their conversation, using a different colour for each. You are only an observer, so cannot ask questions—you only write what they are saying to each other (or what they are thinking). Once they say good-bye to each other. Close your eyes again, breathe in, with a long breath out. Just be quiet and mindful while you slowly bring yourself back into the present.

Re-read what you wrote—having listened to this conversation as a neutral onlooker, you will probably see a different point of view than what you saw before.

Take the time you need to mourn and create a structure—defining your questions, forming new habits, changing your perspective, revising your beliefs, regular mirror talks, writing your emotions and thoughts into your journal—to cope with what has happened and allow yourself to heal.

Be gentle and patient with yourself, love yourself, honour yourself and respect who you are.

To learn more, visit: www.yournewbeginningbook.com

9

One Step at a Time— Looking Forward

When one door of happiness closes, another opens; but often we look so long at the closed door that we do not see the one which has been opened for us."
                                                —Helen Keller

Past—Present—Future

Y OUR LIFE CONSISTS of your past, your present and your future. Well, in reality, your past is history, your present is all you really have and your future is dictated by what you learned from the past and how you use this to determine what you want in your life. Sound complicated?

The reason why I'm including this important component of you, is to establish your place here. Many people ask themselves why they are on the planet. Maybe you have, but maybe you've never bothered to think this way. In reality, if you want to find yourself in the haystack of life—it can be a difficult task.

We're going to look back to the past just for a short while . . .

You have events in your life that stand out as specific milestones that you remember because of the effect on you.

You will find that you have shoved several of these into a distant back corner of your mind. Mostly forgotten, secret or hidden, these can be recalled, with help and much internal contemplation, pertinent to either success or 'sitting in a mud-puddle.'

Some large and small incidents in your life are floating close to the surface, and pop into your conscious mind easily and quickly. These may serve you in a negative or a positive way, with a noticeable impact on who you are and how you perceive your life.

Unfortunately when somebody close to you is no longer here, you have to do a lot of digging around to make sense of what your life is going to be like now. What you may consider as uninteresting, trivial facts and experiences in your life, could help you to make some sense of where you are now and how you can deal with this distressing event.

Only once you have done a bit of the searching, can you plan and make a decision about some areas of your life. Some may be completely intact, while others are totally out of kilter, others may be too hurtful, stressful, or painful—or occurrences that you simply choose to ignore.

As you know, we cannot destroy memories. However, the way that we use them in our present lives can be changed.

Get out of the loft of your memories and use these to better yourself.

This could mean that you have to re-visit times in your life that dishearten you, times that make you wonder why you didn't act differently and times that you know were not uplifting for you. (Refer to Chapter 5.4 pg 127)

Now you can re-structure and re-write them to make you stronger to tackle the way forward.

This may be just what you need to find what you want, what you really, really want.

The Spice Girls keep asking you—so—ask yourself:

> *Yo, I'll tell you what I want, what I really, really want*
>
> *So tell me what you want, what you really, really want*
>
> *I'll tell you what I want, what I really, really want*
>
> *So tell me what you want, what you really, really want . . .*

Just give vent to what you want, without limits and write freely without limiting yourself..

You can even draw what you want.

While you write or draw . . . sing along if you want.

To learn more, visit: www.yournewbeginningbook.com

Dreams

Like Susan Boyle, when she stood on that stage, saying she wanted to be a singer, she started singing—'I dreamed a dream' . . . and the rest you know.

What an amazing story—from Dream to Reality! She knew what she wanted, she had the passion, the drive, the courage and the cheek to get up there and do what she wanted, what she really, really wanted.

You, too, can live your dream. With it comes your passion for what you want, the reason why you want it, and the action to get it. If Susan had not walked onto that stage, she would still be where she was before.

Are you too scared to take a step in the direction that you want? If something is holding you back, pause for a minute . . .

Do This:

You have already achieved much in your life.

Instead of focusing on your failures or fears, spend some time recording your previous successes.

Your subconscious will help you with this.

Write your ideas so you can Find Your Dream.

Here's an opportunity for you to grow and find the real you.

If you have one or a few great dreams that you've had for a long time, you are at the starting line now. So be ready, get set and see yourself achieving this!

Take stock of your ambitions, skills and opportunities that you have to make a dream come true. Below, write single words of the actions you can take to start living your dream.

_____

_____

_____

Go back to the box and the lines above, and, using your colours, number them in order of importance—for you to achieve one small realistic dream. Keep it small and simple enough to get started on this journey. If your dream is too big, it may take a long time to achieve, and if you are still feeling fragile, be patient and take little steps, one at a time

The circle below is your Dream Circle. Take a second, close your eyes and decide what would work best for you—working from the outside inwards, or from the inside outwards.

Now number them this way and add your dream words into each consecutive circle—this will give you a visual structure of what you have to do to achieve that dream.

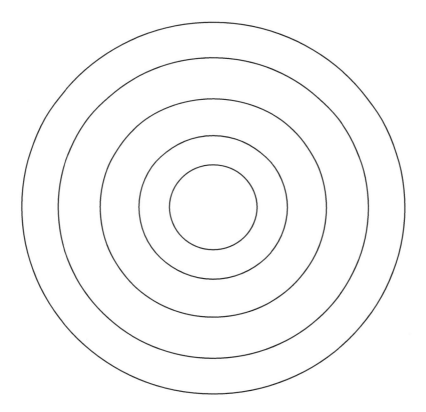

Add some colour into your dream circle.

Next, decide what 'game plan' you want to create.

Be very clever with your strategy, your plans and how you what to achieve these. You can also date them if you want.

My Dream Plan:

Starting Point

To run a race, to reach a goal, you have to start somewhere. You have to know what it entails, the speed at which you want to move to reach your cut-off time, prepare and then accept that you are doing this because it is your choice.

You have a strategy in mind—whether you go full out all the way, hold back a bit up to a certain distance or pace yourself all the way to the end—you know the story of the rabbit and the tortoise.

Create your starting point with a strategy that works for you—one that ensures that you win.

No! Let's re-phrase: your 'race' is really your journey of life.

Consider also: you are the only one on your journey. Yes, there will be some supporters and some spectators, some helpers and some who tell you that you are on the wrong road.

Ultimately, you are completely responsible for yourself to reaching your dream(s).

1. You have to know where you are going—what you want in life.

2. You have to choose a way to get there.

3. You have to add in passion, your senses, your desire and motivation.

4. You have to take the action required to get you where you want to be.

You will win! It is Your Life, Your New Beginning.

Do This:

This is a journey that you should be looking forward to, a journey that brings you closer to the goals you have set for yourself—and as you travel along your chosen path you can have fun, a sense of achievement, smile again and find a happy balance.

Here's to creating your starting point:

Fill in the blanks:

- What 'race/journey' do you want to start?

  _____

- What is your end goal?

  _____

- What are some of the mile-posts along the way?

  _____

- How soon do you have to start?

  _____

- What time target do you want for yourself?

  _____

- What do you want to learn along the way?

  _____

- What do you want to achieve on arrival at your destination?

  _____

- What interesting memories do you want to collect along the way?

  _____

Who won? The rabbit or the tortoise?

Take your time—this is your life—nobody else's. Run it your way.

Goals

To reach a goal, you have to set one. You've got your list of dreams and new things you want to do in your life.

The next step is to take action by setting small, easy-to-achieve goals for yourself. One way is to get out a calendar and write what you want to achieve by a certain date. I've done that so many times—but it didn't really work as I well as I was hoping.

Why?

Well, again, and it sounds like a repetition, but your habits, your consistent thoughts and reminders from your subconscious mind about how to run your life and keep doing what you have been doing to all your life, will cause you to look at it and find all kinds of excuses to not allow it to happen.

Unless you change your old habits! Start new ones to take their place, persist in doing it over and over and over until it starts becoming a new habit.

Even then, you have to *want* to embrace this new habit enough to make it real.

As in a race—you have to want to win it with everything you've got and then run it. So too with the journey that you're embarking on now—you have to want it, desire it, get set, and go for it. Not just a blind race. Oh, and remember the car you wanted!

Taking small steps in the direction of your goal, is the only way.

Moving with more strategic steps, get a large poster board or blank paper, and draw a circle in the middle. Use your colours for this. You are going to draw a mind-map.

Draw a few lines out from the edge of the circle. Write a different goal on each line. Then draw lines from each and write the steps to take for each goal. Keep going until you can see the bigger picture and find yourself dreaming of ways to accomplish what you want.

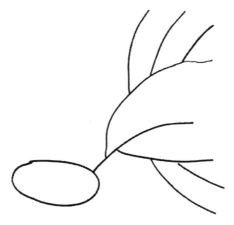

To learn more, visit: www.yournewbeginningbook.com

Reality Check

Why a reality check? Well, you have been doing everything a certain way your whole life. You have been confronted with a huge change now and you know that this is the only way forward.

Keep checking up on yourself. Not to judge, criticise or berate yourself, or to stop yourself in your tracks because those little voices in your head have told you that you are crazy to go into an enchanted forest of the unknown . . . No!

Keep checking up on yourself to encourage yourself, to let you know that you trust your judgement, to motivate yourself to keep moving in the new direction you have chosen. To ensure that, as you want to try something new and different, you can gently persuade yourself that a slight change is OK. You have to keep checking up on yourself with trust and acceptance.

Become proud of who you are, that you are getting things done and that you are dealing with your loss.

Tell yourself that you love yourself, honour yourself and respect yourself.

I'm sure that you've heard of affirmations—you keep saying specific phrases over and over to yourself—until you start believing them and they become your reality.

Definition: Affirmation: *the assertion that something exists or is true; something that is affirmed; a statement or proposition that is declared to be true; confirmation or ratification of the truth or validity of a prior judgment, decision.*

Does this really work? Well, with respect—most of the time—NO! Unless you change your subconscious thoughts, perceptions, values, beliefs and actions.

Why I am being so 'contrary'?

Well, there is another word that I find works much better than just a repetition of something that is the opposite to what your subconscious is willing to believe:

Definition: Intention: *an act or instance of determining mentally upon some action or result; the end or object intended; purpose; the act or choice of intending; meaning or significance.*

Looking at the difference between these two words, the word 'intention' has more of a ring to: 'choosing to do something' rather than simply repeating it over and over. It also informs your subconscious that you want to do something different to what you did before. Add your desire and passion to the pot and you have an assertive, self-conversation of: "Subconscious, this is what I intend to be/do from now on".

Do This:

You want to create different thoughts, actions, perceptions and you are instructing your subconscious mind to take it on as a new reality. Much more powerful!

Right? Got it?

Now take some time and choose 1 intention to have for the week.—that's right—only 1 for the week.

Remember this is a process that needs to be ingrained into your subconscious library that you cannot change overnight. One step at a time. e.g. my intention for today is to drink 8 classes of water.

Your commitment: My intention for today is

_____

_____

Write this onto 5 Post-It notes and put them in 5 places that you will see in one day. E.g. the mirror where you brush your teeth, on the coffee container, in your diary, on the fridge door, and on the steering wheel of your car. Every time you see it, say it 3 times to yourself—aloud if you can and say it with passion.

Do this for 28 days to form you new habit and add it into your progress tracker—Refer to Chapter 2.6 pg 39

To learn more, visit: www.yournewbeginningbook.com

Vision Board

I'm sure you've heard of a vision board. It's the latest craze and everybody is doing them. Do they really work? Well, I had a lady call me and tell me that she had been to seven workshops and made seven vision boards, but none of it was working for her. She asked me if I could help her to get it to work—she did not want to make another one!

The problem was that she had found pictures and words about her dreams, without considering that her subconscious voices would remind her that this was unrealistic—just a dream and not possible to achieve. She had also not cleaned out the library of life experiences that made her who she is, with her subconscious programmed to ensure that she stays this way.

Creating a display of dreams without the inner work to change your subconscious mind-set, could lead to disappointment.

Just imagine—your subconscious starts laughing at you, saying: "Ha, Ha Ha! How do you think you're going to get that? Are you kidding? You have a poverty mind-set and there's no way you can get that—forget it, mate!"

Disappointment and disillusionment then set in and mostly these dreams stay exactly what they are—a poster board with pictures of your dreams.

If you are wondering if I think that vision boards *do not work,* you are wrong. They are extremely effective if you do them in the right way. Many successful people swear by them—Oprah Winfrey, and Ellen DeGeneres among others.

I created a very specific vision board about two years before writing this book—done the way I just described. I followed a precise method of chucking out old BS that I didn't want in my life any longer and started taking action to realise some of my 'visions'. As we all know, Rome wasn't built in a day, so it's taken some time to reap the results. Some of my dreams have already come to fruition, some not yet. Some have changed, but I know that I will be able to realise my dreams—my Vision Board is one of the tools I use to being able to accomplish them.

Firstly, you have to get rid of the old BS, set new intentions, take action and only then, step-by-step, can changes start to happen for you. If you want to start creating one—go ahead!

Because it is a visible representation of your dreams—like your little important Post-It's all over your environment—your senses bring it to your attention consistently.

The saying: "What you see is what you get!" works in this way. Just do It!

To learn more, visit: www.yournewbeginningbook.com

Get Creative—Get Active—Get Your Life Sorted

Looking back continually at your past, is like sitting in that mud puddle. You'll get nowhere fast—or at all. You will start wondering what life is all about, why you are in this predicament, start doubting yourself and wondering how the hell you can get out of your hell.

To activate your energy, again you have limitless choices.

1. Get creative:

   - Buy some flowers that appeal to you and arrange them in that vase that's been sitting in the bottom of your cupboard.

   - Get some paints, paint brushes and paint a picture.

   - Put music on and dance to your heart's content for hours.

   - Sing as loud as you want in the shower or in the car.

   - Write that poem or story that's been in the back of your head forever.

   - Paint your friend's nails.

   - Up-cycle some old clothes or shoes and wear them with your creative twist.

   - Paint that piece of furniture that has been bothering you for a while.

   - Create the most amazing dessert you can think of.

   - Change your hair style.

- Cut out pictures and create a collage of pretty things in that old frame and hang it in the empty space on your wall.
- Bake a cake and ice it.

2. Get active:

- Take yourself on a quick walk.
- Tomorrow, a longer, slower walk on a different route.
- Go for your free trial of a Pilates or Zumba class.
- Join a salsa group.
- Go on a window-shopping adventure when the shops are closed.
- Go fly a kite in the park.
- Take your neighbour's dog for a walk (ask them first).
- Instead of by bus or in your car—walk to the library, or somewhere you'd like to go.
- Play hop-scotch on the pavement blocks.
- Wash your car by hand.
- Clean the windows of your house—inside & out.
- Have a picnic in the park and walk around after eating.
- Park your car a few blocks away from the shops, or get off the bus a few stops early.

- Ride your bike around the block a few times.
- Walk up the stairs instead of taking the lift.

3. Get your life sorted.

  - Just do what you've got to do.
  - Join friends or groups to do different activities.
  - Make new friends.
  - Be kind to yourself.
  - When you feel emotional, let it out and send it on its way.
  - Use your intention Post-Its to remind yourself of who you are.
  - Create new habits.
  - Embrace change—do not fear it.
  - Take self-doubt by the ears and throw it out of the window.
  - Be a kid again.
  - Do something daring.
  - Try one new thing a week.
  - Be patient with yourself but push yourself—just a little nudge is perfect.
  - Keep moving towards your goals.
  - Focus on healing.
  - Get out of that mud-puddle.
  - Trust yourself.

- Know you can.
- Believe in yourself.

Never look back. Keep your eyes on the positive. Laugh until your stomach hurts. Go and watch a comedy.

This is your responsibility.

If you have children, get them to work through this book with you and help them to understand the implication of this major event on their lives. You owe it to them to guide them through the process too.

Make it special and a fun time.

To learn more, visit: www.yournewbeginningbook.com

10

Your New Beginning

Pearls don't lie on the seashore. If you want one, you must dive for it.

—Chinese proverb

So, let's start at the very beginning . . .

Nobody Else Can Do It For You

YES, YOU ARE at a turning point in your life right now. You had that special person with whom you shared your thoughts, you did things together and were simply there for each other. This person is no longer around and the most important factor is that you have to accept this as a given. Sadly this cannot be changed.

Take responsibility for your life. Your friends, family and support groups were and are there for you, however, they have to get on with their lives too—the good news is that you are now in charge of your own life.

Work through the steps of dealing with your loss and repeat whenever they pop up onto your path.

Remember that *you* are in control of *you*—nobody else. Tongue in cheek: Mind Your Own Business!

You will be OK if you Just Do It!

Be Comfortable with Yourself

You are who you are, and you have only yourself to contend with. You have no choice but to live with you. You have no choice but to accept yourself unconditionally.

Others may mean well by telling you how to run your life, but when they leave, you're stuck in their confusion and doubt, uncertain of your next step. Their judgements are from their point of view. Their way of dealing with life and how they would act, react and respond to external events in their lives, is also from their perspective.

It's important for you to get back into your own shoes, into your own life and get comfortable with who you are, who you want to be and where you are headed to on your journey.

It's all up to you. If you're unsure, have a stern talk with your subconscious, telling it that you are now comfortable with being in change, and ask it to get out of the way.

Learn the value of yourself. Stand back, get out of your own way and allow yourself to be you. Get comfortable with who you are.

To learn more, visit: www.yournewbeginningbook.com

Be Courageous

It takes courage to stand up to yourself—emotionally, mentally, physically, creatively and spiritually.

If you're aware and mindful of whom you are, it becomes easier to find your way through the obstacles that arrive in your path. No, it's not all easy, and it takes some courage to decide that you're OK.

You are this far in the book. Be grateful to yourself that you've been tenacious in getting here. Acknowledge this, look in the mirror and congratulate yourself.

If you think you can, you know you can—just do it without question.

You've been resolute in learning to deal with your loss. Now use this determination on your way forward.

Say Yes to Yourself

At times, your subconscious may be so strong that it over-rules and wants to force you to back in the direction you habitually thought and reacted. You are more aware of those little voices telling you what they think you should be doing—either because this is what you've always done, or maybe because others expect certain behaviour or actions from you.

By now you are taking steps and making decisions regularly to choose and do what you're determined to do—by looking at unconventional ways to heal, to deal with your loss and to re-gain your life.

Give yourself a great resounding Yes. Say YES to the changes you want in your life.

Speak now! Say Yes to yourself. Give yourself permission! Just Do It!

When That Flood Arrives . . .

It is inevitable. The floodgates of emotion do not ask permission to attack. Like when the weather gets really stupid and there's a freak storm—it just happens, and there's nothing you can do about it. You have to sit tight and ride out the storm.

As this part of the healing process arrives without any notification, you may wonder what the reason is for this re-occurrence of shock. There probably isn't one.

Yes, just sit tight, allow the storm to pass and know that you'll feel lighter afterwards. Be mindful that you are working through this part of your grief and that your subconscious has dealt you a few more pent-up emotions. That's OK! It's making a space for happier emotions to fill that gap.

Enjoy the storm. Be mindful of the clouds, the thunder, the downpour and the tears of sadness. Allow it to wash over you and let it run away down the path you are walking on— So be it!

Ride it out, walk in the rain, look into the clouds and see the silver lining, re-fresh your energies and smell the new clean air after the dust has been cleared.

Combat Exhaustion

Exhaustion, depression and despondency and burnout can manifest in a whirlpool, dragging you further down into the doldrums—a state of mind that becomes more difficult to get out of.

Maybe you don't usually run your life like this, but when it hits you sideways, remember the song: 'I get knocked down, but I get up again'.

You are here now. Make the most of your life in the present and on your journey forward.

Many varying factors can cause you to crawl before you can stand steadily on your feet. That's fine! Keep moving—it's the only way forward.

Simply keep going until you get to a place where you don't feel down anymore.

If frustration, pain and confusion persist, combat that sensation of being pulled down at the speed of a tornado, by writing. Grab our journal and write until it's all out of your system.

Writing moves your energy. It provides a step out of a consuming vortex of pain, frustration and exhaustion.

Take a few minutes right now—sit quietly, re-balance and know that you are OK. Choose again to regain your life. (Ref Chapter 4.2 pg 78)

You are taking responsibility for your own healing. Other people do not know exactly how you feel and what you're going through. This is your life. Ask yourself what lesson you can learn from what has happened.

You've got the power within yourself to notice your feelings, to acknowledge the symptoms of the storm, to re-assure your subconscious that you are in control and then start using the tools you have to combat a state of fatigue. Just Do It!

Ground Yourself & Connect to Nature

You are a part of the Universe—a part of nature and nature is part of you.

Ground yourself—smell the flowers, walk barefoot on the smooth grass, touch the bark of a tree and look closely at the details of a leaf. Stop and listen to the birds, put your face into the sun and drink in the sunlight. Sing to your heart's content. Walk in the park and be that cherished detail of nature that you really are—an amazing person.

Put this book down now, go out and do it!

Be Mindful

1. Pay attention.

2. Use your senses.

3. Be aware of your thoughts.

4. Ignore the past and avoid the future—bring yourself into the now.

5. Be quiet.

6. Pay attention (on purpose) to this very moment without judgement.

You've plucked up the courage, said yes to yourself, weathered your emotions, grounded yourself and brought this all into your consciousness—this is a huge step forward.

You are becoming a new you with a new way of living. Do it every day. Make it your habit and embrace the transformation.

Manage your Experiences

Your mindfulness is assisting you to 'experience' your experiences. Take note of which thoughts, emotions, self-talk and self-questions are driving you—some wanted and some unwanted.

When you work with a difficult experience like this one, you have to take charge of your subconscious mind—you can manage it like a business—where you are the boss.

Actually—you are your own boss. How are you going to treat yourself? How would you like to be treated? Answer these two questions from a different point of view. Tell your subconscious to go and *&%$—because you're no longer taking instructions from your history. You're starting a new life now—being treated the way you have always *wanted* to be treated.

Do this for you! You owe it you yourself to be treated with respect, with trust, with honour—nothing less!

It's all up to you—be the little blue engine: think you can, know you can and be grateful that you 'can'.

Accept the Things You Cannot Change

Maybe you are struggling with or resisting acceptance of this situation in your life. Mindfulness is an avenue to connect yourself to reality.

What if . . . ? If only . . . ? But why . . . ? Why me . . . ?

The questions you ask yourself will give you answers from your experiences. You will only get partial answers to a reality that does not exist, or answers that do not help you to move forward.

You have two options:

1. You can sit in a mud puddle, feeling sorry for yourself, stirring the mud round and round, focusing so much on the mud that you can't see a way out—you can wallow in your own misery...

   Or

2. You can accept that there are things that you cannot change, grab the bull by the horns and get on with your life—create a new beginning for yourself.

Imagine that, right now there is a knock on your door and two policemen have a warrant for your arrest—you get rushed off and locked up and spend the night in a prison cell.

You've been arrested because you are balancing your life on a dangerously high tightrope.

How will you react?

Frederick Langbridge wrote this for us to learn a very important lesson about ourselves:

> "Two men look through the self-same bars; one sees the mud, the other sees the stars."

Which one are you?

Notice the Good Things—Let Them In

There are so many positive things happening around you. Are you aware of them, or are you focused on the negative?

Lift yourself out of the quick-sand by taking action.

Inspect each aspect of your life to find even the tiniest details of something for which you can be grateful. No matter how small, it has an effect on you and, if you pay attention to these insignificant, positive features, they will grow bigger and bigger, until one day you will wake up and think: 'Wow! Life is Great!' 'I'm OK!'

Find the little, beautiful, details surrounding you, let them in, nurture them, pamper them. Then notice how they thrive, expand and grow into powerful components that keep you motivated, help you heal and bring you joy.

Learn to Choose

One of the reasons to practice mindfulness and acknowledge gratitude—no matter how irrelevant you thought they were—is that it gives you a wider choice. Not a choice of what happens to you, but a new personal choice of your responses, reactions and perceptions.

It is natural to go into physical shock when you experience an incident that pushes you out of your comfort zone. The way you deal with every situation will be automatic.

'Mindfulness' and being aware of how you think and perceive your circumstances, will broaden your understanding of yourself. It will lead you to a more disciplined way of responding to your emotions—a way that gives you what you want for yourself.

This means that you can learn to choose what feedback you want to send to your subconscious, which ultimately affects your auto-responses.

You can choose to change and 'be in the present moment'. And you can choose your thoughts. Do you choose to worry or to be happy?

You know that song by Bobby McFerrin: "Don't Worry—Be Happy"?

Sing it now—loud and clear.

Choose it whenever you start to worry. Sing it while you embrace change!

Learn to choose new habits. Learn to choose new thoughts. Learn to choose a new perspective and learn to make new choices.

Decide to choose what you want while learning to cope with any inconsistencies that arise.

To learn more, visit: www.yournewbeginningbook.com

Be Kind to Yourself

All the expectations that you're confronted with now, can be rather overwhelming. Remember that Rome wasn't built in a day. Your subconscious mind is pushing you in one direction while the change you want may be pulling you in a different direction.

With the subsequent changes that have taken your life by storm—create some me-time for yourself. If something doesn't get done today—it's OK. You will find your own time to cope with what has happened. The unconventional point of view keeps you focused on the present, changing your perspective on the future by re-visiting your past experiences, beliefs, habits and choices.

Be kind to yourself and start moving away from the extreme pain to a place where you can feel that you are healing.

All the changes that you have thought about—find your starting point and take the first step. A small step is still moving in the right direction. Strike while the iron is hot—with the dramatic change in which you find yourself now, why wait to start making small changes to help you deal with your life in a different way? Steer yourself in the direction you want to go!

If you are afraid of change—you're in it—so go with the flow and head for happiness. Move toward a positive place instead of hanging on to regrets, pain, misery and total abandon. Do this with great consideration for yourself.

Be kind to yourself by giving yourself the time you need, yet, be assertive, focused and caring in the way you talk to yourself. Step outside of yourself and give yourself advice from your new perspective, in spite of insecurities, doubts and questions that come with change. Just do it.

Be gentle with yourself. Be unique. Take yourself away from others if you want to be alone. Watch, listen and learn from others. Be comfortable with your own company. Be quiet and mindful, and know who you want to be. Embrace you desires.

Go out and test-drive your new vehicle of life. Love yourself again—unconditionally. Tell yourself that you will be OK and Smile!

Shape Up For Life

Colouring exercise for you. Today, colour each of these in the suggested colours:

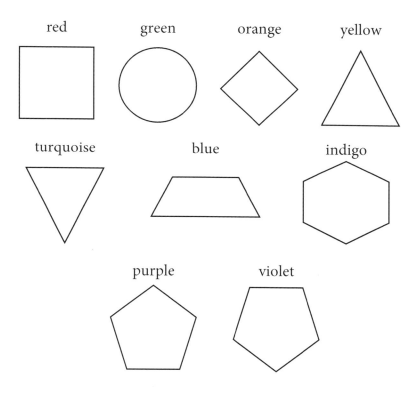

red   green   orange   yellow

turquoise   blue   indigo

purple   violet

At any time when you're feeling really low and struggling to move on, come back to these shapes.

Simply focus on the first one that you see when you look at them all. Stare at that one for a few minutes. Close your eyes, empty out all other thoughts in your head and the colour will appear in your mind's vision. Enjoy that shape and colour till it fades into the distance. Take a deep breath in and long slow breath out before you open your eyes.

Remind yourself that you are shaping up for a new beginning.

To learn more, visit: www.yournewbeginningbook.com

Your New Beginning

In conclusion, I'd like to share this story with you from nature.

Sitting on a mulberry leaf in a very tall tree is Missy, a very pretty little caterpillar. She has no idea though, that she's good looking and has no airs or graces about her. She loves to draw pictures of butterflies and paint them in beautiful bright colours.

She loves poetry, and her favourite one is:

Flitter, flutter, butterfly,

Can I catch you if I try?

Flitter over all the flowerbeds,

Flutter high above our heads,

Bye-Bye, butterfly!

She's very popular with peers and adults alike. She's very intelligent and secures all the most prestigious awards at school. She has everything going for her as she earns lead roles in school pantomimes, attains gold medals in dance competitions, and is an all round athletic champion, excellent tennis player, not to mention her artistic and musical talents which give her many opportunities to be very successful.

Saying this, her brothers and sisters, a number of her friends, other students and neighbours are becoming increasingly jealous of her. Through her artistic endeavours, her parents are becoming more concerned that she's not doing what they think she should do—become a teacher.

She is being kept in tow by her parents. They've convinced her that she cannot earn money from being an artist, even though this was her dream from a very young age. She's given up the theatre and dance careers as they have the same perception about these. In fact, she decides that she will quietly just pretend to be what they want her to be. So she starts retreating into a special place that she has found—at the outer end of a crooked branch there's a small cave-like hiding place, umbrella'd by large, strong leaves sheltering the entrance. She takes time out every day, goes for a long 'walk' to her private hiding place where she can paint, draw, sing, be herself and sit in wonder at the beauty of the butterflies.

More and more often, she takes a step back and sits in the corners, watching listening, learning and just being quiet on the side.

After her amazing formative years pointing to a very successful life, in contrast, Missy habitually withdraws from being out there in the front—a successful leader. She retreats into a quiet life of being in the audience instead of on stage. Even though she knows who she really is, she becomes an onlooker. She knows in her heart of hearts that this is not the real Missy.

By now she's receded to the extent that she prefers to eat the smaller healthy leaves instead of the big crunchy ones. She spends most of her time in her hideout. She's healthy but considerably smaller than most of the other caterpillars around her. She likes to be different but in a non-contradictory way. Strangely, she's completely appreciative of who she really is, and at times, lives this out when she's around a few other caterpillars who appreciate her for who she is.

One rainy, dull day, she's out on a different branch and meets some caterpillars who she doesn't know. When they start talking to her, they acknowledge her. They accept her and are in awe of what they learn from her in their discussions. It's such a wonderful day for her. She's extremely sad when darkness draws in and she has to return home. So she goes back to being obscure and excluded. She has become used to it, but vividly recalls the excitement of being free to be who she really is.

The weather starts to warm up and, while in hiding under a very big leaf, she notices a luscious, ripe mulberry. With its sweet aroma wafting past her nose, she closes her eyes and moves closer. Um, she thinks—I know we don't eat these, but this one is soooo smooth, smells soooo delicious, I think I'm going to just lick it to see if it's ok.

Wow, the taste takes her to a place she's never been. It's tantalising and magic. So she dares a wee bite out of one little mulberry bud. Scrumptious! That's it! The smallest, most tender leaves didn't come close to this delightful flavour. She eats a bit more and a bit more. Where she's hiding, nobody can see or comment about what she's doing.

She's so inspired by what she's learning. She realises that she's supposed to explore new things and she loves the adventure of mystery. She believes that she's setting herself up for something awesome. She looks around but decides to still keep her secret to herself. She's done this all her life—she's not suddenly going to change this.

Life goes on as all the caterpillars grow up, eat more leaves and bulk out substantially.

Then one morning, after having a breakfast of mulberries quietly under the broad leaves, she ventures out into the big wide world and notices that some of the other caterpillars have started spinning cocoons. Some of them deliver gleaming silver-white silk from their mouths, automatically spinning a small enclave around them. Others produce stunning saffron-yellow silk which shines like pure gold in the sun. Others liberate amber, cream or ivory shades of magnificent thread.

Wow, she thinks—that's really beautiful and interesting.

One of the oldest caterpillars in the tree sees her admiring the spinning and wobbles over to chat with her. He looks at her with great regard and speaks in a quiet voice—one that she can relate to. And this is what he says:

"Being silkworms gives us a purpose in life—we create the most beautiful fabric in the world—pure silk. Even though we're all here together, heading toward the same destination, we also each have our own journey, our own strengths, and our own uniqueness—to enrich the world with our special gift from nature:

Something soft to touch and beautiful to admire, something with exclusive ingredients to counteract ageing, something stronger than steel, yet so delicate that precious gemstones can be wrapped in it and with aesthetic qualities that adorn royalty."

Wow again. This makes her feel important, thinking that she too may have a purpose in life. She sashays off to witness, in fascination, how some of her peers have already started spinning themselves into little oval shapes.

She wonders if she'll be doing the same.

One-by-one all the other caterpillars enclose themselves inside the magical material. One-by-one they drop off to sleep for a while.

Then, being one of the last ones standing, she starts savouring what is pretty much the last mulberry on the tree, enjoying the tingle on her lips.

Suddenly she experiences a strange sensation in her cheeks, a feeling like she's on some potion-induced trip. She waits in anticipation. Will this sensitivity mean a breakthrough? Will she also be able to spin a cocoon of beautiful pure silk?

Her thoughts race! What would her silk look like? Would anybody want to use her silk for a spectacular, stunning garment? Will her threads adorn a princess? Or would it just be the same as all the others? Either way, it's still a mystical form of nature, a gift from her to the world.

As the urge to wipe her mouth after her delectable breakfast becomes overbearing, she picks up a soft young leaf to dust off any leftover juice on her lips to ensure her secret is still safe with her.

At the end of her leafy napkin she sees something shiny. She takes a closer look—it's a single thread of silk. A gentle but exquisitely gorgeous pink colour. She hasn't seen anything like it—ever. She's over the moon. She wants to shout out to everybody about her creation. At long last it's her turn. Yet, automatically she conceals her secret yet again.

A fine rose filament is flowing from her lips and she's enjoying the sensation of sharing what she's had from a very young age—her unique gift to the world. It just pours out with abandon, wrapping her in the silkiest, softest bed she's ever had. She closes her eyes as she moves around, forming an opulent enclosure. For a moment she stops to take a look at what she's achieving. She gasps at the beauty—her cocoon is spectacular, soft pink. Wow, she's so pleased that she ate those mulberries—what a result!

With this incredible sense of success, she realises that her silk is coming to an end, and she's becoming quite sleepy. She's so grateful that she can sleep in such a charming cocoon . . .

She knows she has to sleep for a while and that she'll be transformed into a moth—just like all the other silkworms. She is excited, yet not sure of her future.

She thinks back on her life and those around her.

She'd watched them struggle for survival, strive to be better than others, compete to exhaustion, fit into the system of daily routines. Some of them had fought and been knocked off the branches and fallen to the ground. Some were arrogant and had lost their balance strutting around, hitting the ground with a thud. Some had not looked after themselves and become old and shrivelled and weren't able to spin big cocoons. Some greedy ones had gorged themselves so they couldn't reach all the way around themselves, resulting in incomplete cocoons. Some cheeky ones had tried to sneak into the cocoons of others. There were others who had lovely cocoons, just doing life as it came to them, happy to just plod along.

She's happy with who she is, so she places her head on the small, soft pillow inside her little home and closes her eyes. She's excited, yet not sure of what lies ahead. She allows herself to drift off . . . far away into a dream.

As she falls asleep in her bed of delicate silk, she dreams that when she wakes up, she'll be different and able to tell the world the message she has inside her—the one she's learned to hide while watching the other silkworms.

Then, one day her dream changes and it seems to be calling her to wake up. She listens, but before opening her eyes, she takes a long, deep breath.

Wow, it warms her lungs and she knows that a new day has arrived. Slowly she opens her eyes. She's still snuggled into her cocoon. She also knows that this is a place she no longer wants to be in.

She pushes her elbows against the sides, hoping it will just break open. It's too strong to give way. She tries to peep to the outside, but there are too many strands for her to see anything. She comes to the conclusion that she has to claw and cut herself out of her enclosure. She knows it may be a struggle, but she's inspired to take action soon—she has to get out of here . . . .

She squeezes her tiny fingers between the strands to push them aside, but they are firmly embedded and will not budge. She exerts all her energy and a few strands move. She persists because she can hear a flutter of wings and sighs of relief as some other silkworms manage to crawl out of their cocoons.

She's determined to get out as soon as possible because she's starting to feel claustrophobic. She pushes and shoves, uses her teeth to pull some fibres to the side. She is alone with nobody to assist. She is finding it really tiresome to cope with moving this enveloping cage. At times she just wants to give up. She doesn't know what's on the other side anyway. She's considering calling for help, but everybody is busy with their own life. She knows that she has to do this, but the little voices in her head keep telling her that she's in her hiding place anyway—why bother.

She cries, she tries and then, as she has to make a decision to whether she should continue the hard work to break free, she rests for a few seconds. The one area has become thin enough for the sun to shine through in little warm rays. She realises that she's forgotten who she really is. She's been so focused on this encroaching feeling of survival that she's not noticed and forgotten something really important . . . She's surrounded by dazzlingly beautiful pink silk.

This gives her a reason to deal with all the basic complexities of breaking free—a reason to change her thoughts and perceptions that are potentially stopping her from getting out of the 'mud puddle' that her subconscious is suggesting to her.

Gathering all her energy with one last surge, she uses every bit of her strength to push through the thinner area that she'd taken so long to clear . . .

Her head pops through the hole and out of her confinement.

She views her surroundings. Oh! She's still in the same tree. Around her are dozens of silvery-coloured moths, stretching their fluffy wings and preening their feather-like 'antennae'. She smiles.

As she looks at herself, she sees that her front legs have developed into pretty legs. She uses these new appendages to hold onto the blush-coloured bed she's been sleeping in and pulls her body out in one fell swoop.

What a relief!

She'd thought she could do this and now she knows she can. She had been squeezed in so tightly that she could hardly breathe, but now her lungs are free to take in the fresh air. She takes a long deep breath. She smiles. She has an unfamiliar feeling on her back and realises that these are her wings. She can't see what they look like but has the instinctive urge to stretch out that part of her body. She's very patient with herself and does this gently. She feels like something spectacular is happening. This area of her body stretches and grows and spreads out and unfolds—like nothing she's ever experienced before. It's an incredible feeling.

As she looks around, she sees the other moths staring at her in amazement. She sees the look on their faces and wonders what is happening to her? Should she just go and hide again, like she always has?

She hears a few 'Wow's from the crowd. The hushed whisperings that she was used to are different now. Some of her moth friends are flying closer to look at her. They are looking at her with admiration, respect, in awe and adoration. Oops! Why?

One friendly moth whispers in her ear: 'Wow! Who are you? You always hid behind those leaves, so we never noticed you much . . . but now we can see . . .'

'What do you mean?' Missy asks. 'Just go and look at yourself in the mirror', her friend prompts her.

With difficulty, she pulls her inept body over to a mirror. There, reflecting back at her, are spectacular, brightly coloured patterns, rising up behind her head, in perfect symmetry, waiting in anticipation for a new exciting venture.

She's been transformed into a resplendent butterfly.

She spreads her wings and feels herself being lifted up . . . she flits over the flowerbeds, then flutters high above their heads . . .

Only you can transform you life.

Allow yourself to know that you can deal with your loss. Find out who you really are. Decide and choose who you want to be. Do everything you have to do, to find your true

amazing self amidst the rough branches of your life . . . Find
your New Beginning.

Flitter, flutter, butterfly!
Can I catch you if I try?
Flitter o'er the flower beds.
Flutter up above our heads!
Bye, bye butterfly!
Flitter, flutter, butterfly!
Flutter high, Flutter low,
Flutter fast, flutter slow
Flitter flutter butterfly,

Fly on through the deep blue sky!